Life in the Quality Lane

The LifeSkills To Make Each Moment Matter

Dudley Weeks, Ph.D.

Copyright © 2011 Dudley L. Weeks

Printed by CreateSpace

Website: http:www.dudleyweeks.com

Email author at: booksandmusic@dudleyweeks.com

This book may be purchased at:
www..createspace.com/3491828

All rights reserved. This book may not be reproduced in whole or in part or transmitted in any form or by any means —mechanical or electronic—without written permission from the author, except by a reviewer who may quote brief passages in a review.

All names other than the author's have been changed to protect the privacy of clients. The examples in the book are, however, based on real situations.

ISBN-13 978-1453883310
ISBN-10 1453883312

Introduction

On the road of life there are several lanes. The fast lane, the slow lane, the speed limit lane, even the shoulder lane we wander onto at times. We often veer back and forth, perhaps searching for a different lane, one that helps make our life journey a journey of *quality*. There is such a lane, the Quality Lane, and the book you are holding in your hands can help us find and travel that lane.

Living a life of quality is a goal most people share. Although perceptions of what constitutes a "quality" life may differ somewhat in terms of details, the major ingredients are generally accepted. Being effective, finding happiness, having self-respect and being respected, developing healthy relationships and interactions, being successful....all are among the most critical ingredients of a "quality" life.

As we travel in the Quality Lane, we need signposts.

The Quality Lane is built on a foundation of practical, proven *LifeSkills* we can use in all aspects of life. They are the signposts on our life journey helping us make each mile, each endeavor more effective. Individual relationships are enriched. Families are strengthened. Organizations and businesses become more effective. Communities become more cooperative. Planning produces better outcomes. Conflicts are resolved in a way that results in sustainable, mutual benefits. Each LifeSkill makes its own valuable contribution, and together they combine to create a process that adds quality to everything we do.

In our increasingly complex, specialized and compartmentalized existence, many people incorrectly assume there could not possibly be a set of all-purpose LifeSkills. As you read *Life in the Quality Lane* and explore the six practical and proven LifeSkills presented, I believe you will see how they are indeed applicable to the diverse endeavors of daily life. The LifeSkills are named and explained in ways that help us remember them and use them readily.

The LifeSkills empower us to understand ourselves and others; to assess situations comprehensively; to make wise decisions; to perform our jobs effectively; to conduct our relationships and interactions with quality; to deal with conflicts.....virtually everything we encounter on the road of life.

This book is dedicated to helping each of us travel life's journey in the Quality Lane.

PART 1

The LifeSkills

LifeSkill #1: Focus on the Broader Context
(the "Circle & Dot" LifeSkill)

LifeSkill #2: Focus on "Connectors"

LifeSkill #3: Develop Secure I, Secure Other, Secure We

LifeSkill #4: Clarify

LifeSkill #5: Focus on What Needs To Be Done,
Can Be Done, and How to Do It

LifeSkill #6: Focus on a Quality Process to
Produce Effective Outcomes

Chapter 1

LifeSkill #1:   Focus on the Broader Context

(The Circle & the Dot)

We know.....
   a forest is more
   than just one tree,
   and a leg is more
   than just the knee,
   a song is more
   than just one note,
   and a fleet is more
   than just one boat,
   the Sun is more
   than just one ray,
   and a life is more
   than just one day.....
      Then tell me, please,
         why we sometimes see
            only the Dot in the Circle ?

Life in the Quality Lane

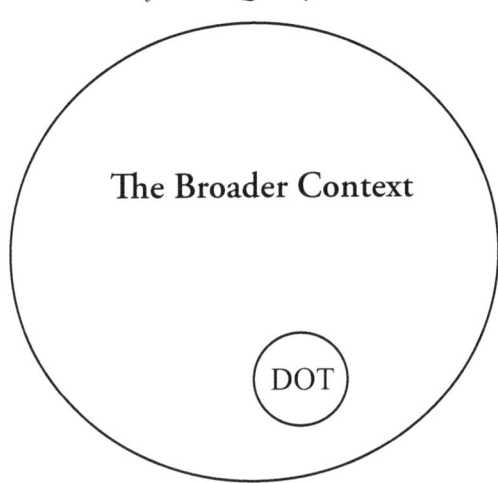

The Circle & the Dot

The diagram of a Dot within a Circle is both simple and profound. The Dot represents any single entity in life, the Circle represents the Broader Context in which that entity exists. There are many important things in the circle besides the Dot but we often become fixated only on the Dot. As in the graphic above, we allow the rest of the Circle to appear empty.

Every person, every situation, every action and interaction, every relationship is more than one of its parts. No matter how strongly we feel about a particular Dot, we need to focus first on the other things that are also within the Circle. Many of them affect and are affected by the Dot, and unless we see the whole picture, we will not be effective.

Keeping the image of the Circle and Dot front and center in our minds can help us in understanding situations, making decisions, designing plans, dealing with problems, buildng effective relationships, interacting with others.....virtually everything we do in life.

Let's look at a few diverse examples of Dots and Circles.

THE DOT	Key Components in the CIRCLE
One component of a person's Identity (gender, beliefs, opinion on an ssue, nationality, etc.)	The WHOLE person, not just one identity component
One negative act	A person's overall behavior, including positive traits

A conflict	The overall relationship or interaction in which a particular conflict occurs
A desire	* How satisfying that desire affects one's own needs and the needs of other people * The means used to satisfy the desire, and if they are consistent with one's own values and ethics
PLANNING: *Planning based only on the best-case outcome. * A planning group focusing only on its design and ignoring the input of those who will be affected by the plan	Planning for various possible outcomes, not only a best-case scenario Including in the design of the plan the input of those who will be affected by the plan
Gaining economic profit	* Ethics * Resource depletion * Excessive accumulation and its effects on the overall economy
Basing a vote only on one issue or solely on political party affiliation	Basing a vote on a more comprehensive assessment of leadership qualities and the needs of the society
Focusing only on outcomes	Also focusing on Process
"Freedom" as doing what I want, when and how I want	"Freedom" as involving responsibility and ethics
One nation's policies	The effects of those policies on the world community
Humanity	The Earth Ecosystem of which humanity is but one component

The Circle and the Dot steps

There are several steps involved in LifeSkill #1, Focus on the Broader Context. The steps help build a foundation on which we can understand situations comprehensively.

<u>STEP 1</u>: Visualize the Circle & Dot image.

<u>STEP 2</u>: Put into the Circle the various components that are important parts of the overall situation.

The Circle represents the complete context of a particular situation (a relationship, an interaction, a challenge, a task.....virtually anything we encounter). Step 2 helps us develop a realistic and comprehensive understanding of the broader context, the "bigger picture".

<u>STEP 3</u>: From among those components, identify the "Connectors".

"Connectors" are things *all* parties involved in a situation consider to be important and/or need. Connectors link people together constructively even though there are things that divide them.

<u>STEP 4</u>: Identify the "Dot(s)". From among the components, identify any that are being fixated on to the exclusion of most everything else in the Circle.

Is the entire situation almost being "defined" by a particular component, resulting in the other components being ignored or viewed as insignificant?

<u>STEP 5</u>: Focus on the other components in the Circle and identify which ones are being ignored, left unfulfilled, or damaged by fixating on the Dot.

This step helps us realize that the Dot we are fixating on is not the only thing that's important in a given situation. There are other things in the Circle we care about, need, and/or want, things that will be obstructed if we fixate on the Dot. Some of those other components in the Circle have a direct influence on, and are directly influenced by, the Dot.

<u>STEP 6</u>: Consider the Dot's relative importance within the

broader context.

In no way does the Circle & Dot LifeSkill imply that the "Dots" in life are unimportant. But *how* important is a particular Dot when seen as but one part of the bigger picture, the broader context? Perhaps it is very important, perhaps it is not as important as we originally thought before we considered the other components in the Circle.

In relationships and interactions, the goal of Step 6 is not to get the parties to agree on the relative importance a particular Dot has to the overall situation. They may agree, they may not, but this step helps them clarify their respective views on how the Dot relates to the bigger picture. This step reduces the tendency to automatically give a Dot more importance than it may deserve in the overall situation.

Taking these six steps can help prepare us with a realistic and comprehensive picture of a situation and its components. That picture gives us a foundation on which we can build an effective process to deal with the situation. Additional skills will be required, of course, primarily the other LifeSkills discussed in this book. They will be covered in subsequent chapters, but for now let's take a specific example and apply the steps of LifeSkill #1. A clear picture of the broader context will result, thereby providing a solid foundation on which to begin dealing effectively with the overall situation.

Example A: The Municipal Improvement Committee (MIC)

The city of Moraville has many problems and unmet needs. Several violent youth gangs are operating, there are only a few small businesses, the city lacks good hospitals and libraries, there is no viable public transportation....the list goes on and on.

To deal with the city's problems, the mayor created the Moraville Improvement Committee five years ago. The MIC is made up of ten Moraville citizens appointed by the mayor, all of whom work for the MIC full time. Since its creation, the MIC has had a good record. Working cooperatively, the members of the MIC have developed nine successful projects, each serving a need of the city.

But now there is a major conflict over how to use a plot of land and a grant given to the city by a wealthy citizen. The donor has offered the land and the money with one stipulation: the MIC must decide on a <u>single</u> project to develop on the land. The MIC immediately splits into two factions, one advocating a health clinic as the project, the other faction advocating a library.

Each faction becomes intensely fixated on its desired project, and a nasty battle ensues. The community is shocked. The members of the MIC have cooperated splendidly with each other in the past, they are personal friends, and several of them have worked together as members of the Parent-Teacher Association at the school attended by their children. But the members are now treating each other as enemies as the library-clinic battle rages.

During the next month, the situation worsens even further. The MIC members engage in behavior unbecoming of responsible leaders. They doggedly try to "win" the battle, and they firmly state they will never agree to the other's project.

Frustrated with the lack of progress, the mayor threatens to disband the MIC, and the donor of the land and money threatens to withdraw the offer. The media covers the sordid battle blow by blow, many citizens of Moraville are calling the MIC a failure, and the MIC members are losing credibility and respect. The mayor finally issues an ultimatum to the MIC: decide on a project at your next meeting or else the MIC will be disbanded and the land and money will be withdrawn. Tanya, one of the MIC members, has recently read *Life in the Quality Lane* and convinces the other members to try the Circle & Dot LifeSkill at their meeting.

(NOTE: Steps 1 and 2 of LifeSkill #1 are presented in the following graphic.)

Step 1: Visualize the Circle & Dot image

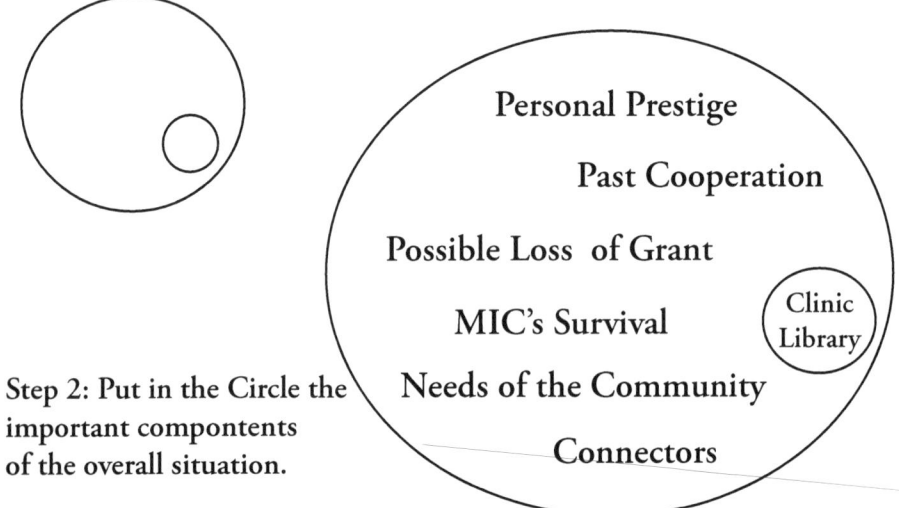

Step 2: Put in the Circle the important compontents of the overall situation.

__STEP 1__: **Visualize the Circle & Dot image.**
Tanya draws the Circle & Dot image on the blackboard and explains that the Circle represents the complete situation and the Dot a particular component among many.

__STEP 2__: **Put into the Circle the various components that are important parts of the overall situation.**
Tanya leads a discussion, asking the MIC members to "fill in" the Circle with the important components of the overall situation. Some of the components the members identity are:
- The welfare of the community and its many needs.
- The continued existence of the MIC and the vital contributions it makes to the community.
- The entire committee has worked well together in the past, overcoming disagreements through effective cooperation.
- Serving on the MIC provides its members with a lot of prestige and influence.
- Meeting one of the community's needs by developing a project on the donated land using the grant money.
- Three key realities of the current situation: (a) the continued existence of the MIC is under threat; (b) the land and money may be withdrawn; and (c) the members of the MIC are losing the respect of the community.
- "Connectors", those things that all parties consider important or needed, things that link them together constructively even though there are things that divide them.

__STEP 3__: **From among those components, identify the "Connectors".**
Tanya explains what "connectors" are, and the members identify the most important connectors as being (a) a shared commitment to the community; (b) shared commitment to the MIC and keeping it alive; (c) their past cooperation and friendship; and (d) they all want to restore their personal prestige and influence as respected leaders.

__STEP 4__: **Identify the "Dot(s)". From among the components, identify any that are being fixated on to the exclusion of most everything else in the Circle.**
It is obvious to all the members that the "Dot" is the fixation on

the project having to be either a clinic or a library. The clinic faction would like to keep thinking the library faction's fixation on the library is the real problem, and the library faction would like to keep thinking the clinic faction's fixation on the clinic is the real problem. But taking Step 4 helps them realize both factions have been choosing to focus on a "Dot" to the exclusion of everything else.

STEP 5: **Focus on the other components in the Circle and identify which ones are being ignored, left unfulfilled, or damaged by fixating on the Dot.**

Three "connectors" (the welfare and needs of the community, the MIC, and prestige as leaders) are identified as suffering most from the impasse created by fixating on the Dot. They all agree those connectors are priority components of the situation.

STEP 6: **Consider the relative importance a particular Dot has within the broader context.**

Tanya asks several questions to help the members take Step 6.

"Did any of you get on the MIC only to get a library or clinic?" (Everybody answers, "No.")

"Is getting a library or clinic on this land with this money more important than keeping the MIC alive, continuing our service to the community, and losing the respect of our fellow citizens?"

(The committee members think, then several say, "No, it's not.")

"Is either faction going to agree to the other faction's project being the one put on this land using this money?" (They answer, "No".)

Then Tanya says, "We have all stated the reason we want to be on the MIC is to develop projects the community needs. Focusing on that shared commitment, let's discuss some other project possibilities. We have worked together cooperatively before, so let's do it now."

Using LifeSkill #1 creates a realistic and comprehensive picture of the overall situation. It serves as an effective foundation on which to move forward in a way that saves the MIC, meets a need of the community, and regains the trust of the citizenry. They will need to use additional skills, of course, and those will be discussed in subsequent chapters.

We now look at other applications of the Circle & Dot. As is true of the MIC case, all examples are taken from actual situations I have encountered in my work. Only the names of the people involved have been changed. The cases presented are quite diverse, demonstrating how this LifeSkill serves as an effective beginning in understanding any situation comprehensively.

The examples could easily be taken from any type of situation, but we will focus on four of the most prevalent types people face in their relationships, interactions, and tasks.

Perceptions of Identity

Our perceptions of ourselves and others have a profound influence on our daily lives.

Who am I? Who are you? How do we view a particular person or group? We have a choice in the way we respond to these questions of "Identity".

The most effective and realistic way is what I call "Holistic Identity". A person's total identity (the Circle) is made up of many components, and we need to perceive and interact with the "total" person, not just "define" that person based on one or a few identity components (Dots).

This graphic shows some of the components of Holistic Identity.

Holistic Identity

The opposite approach is what I will term "Selective Identity", perceiving and treating a person in terms of only one or a few identity components we select to the exclusion of all the others. Selective Identity is not based on reality. *Each person is more than just one or a few components of identity.*

Identity Example

A father (Jason) and his sixteen year old daughter (Chloe) have always had a good relationship. He appreciates and respects her intelligence, concern for others, humor, diligence, and contributions to the family. Then last month she started dating Tomas, a young man her age who is a student at her school. She invites him to have dinner with her family, and to join them on a visit to an amusement park. Jason immediately likes Tomas, far more than any other young man Chloe has dated, and sees many fine qualities in him.

Although Chloe's family is Christian, religion is not high on the list of topics frequently discussed. So another month goes by before Jason finds out Tomas is Muslim. Suddenly, Jason allows a huge "Dot" to consume him. He falls into the trap of Selective Identity, seeing only the Muslim part of Tomas' Holistic Identity. He demands Chloe stop dating Tomas, saying, "No daughter of mine is going to date a Muslim! Muslims can't be trusted!"

Chloe is appalled. She responds by falling into her own Selective Identity trap, perceiving her father only as a religious bigot (her "Dot"). The solid, lifetime father-daughter relationship suffers greatly. Unless they utilize the steps in LifeSkill #1 and move from Selective Identity to Holistic Identity, their relationship will continue to suffer.

Acknowledging the components in the Circle is crucial. Jason needs to see that Tomas is more than just his religion, and that all the positive things Jason originally saw in the young man are still there. For her part, Chloe needs to remind herself that all the admirable qualities she has always seen in her father have not disappeared just because he has allowed what she considers an irrational prejudice to grab hold of him.

How did the things turn out in the actual case? Chloe's mother took the lead in using LifeSkill #1, helping everybody to Focus on the Broader Context. She got Jason and Chloe together and they all discussed how important their relationship was, how good it had always been, how Tomas was more than just his religion, and how Jason was more than just his views on Islam.

Jason realized his attempt to force Chloe to adopt his views on Islam was damaging a major part of his life; namely, his relationship with his daughter. And Tomas realized his friendship with Chloe was much more important than his annoyance over Jason's prejudice. In other words, Tomas' religion gradually ceased to be a "Dot" when the importance of other components in the overall situation was considered.

Keeping the Circle & Dot image in our minds at all times can help us avoid the temptation to fixate on an identity Dot. Religion was the Dot in the Tomas-Jason example, but it could be race, ethnicity, profession, nationality, socio-economic status, a certain personality trait, political party affiliation, opinion on a particular issue....any specific aspect of Identity. By focusing on the Circle, the whole person, we are able to put any single aspect into its proper perspective as but one among many.

This LifeSkill also applies to group identity. Let's say a few members of a particular grouping engage in acts we find deplorable. But the overwhelming majority of the group would never condone or engage in that behavior. We have a choice in how we perceive the group. If we focus only on the Dot (the few people in that group who engage in deplorable behavior), we are apt to make the mistake of perceiving and treating the entire group based on the actions of those few members.

Another category of Circles & Dots focuses on what can be termed The Negative Behavior Pattern. We can also call it the Worst Behavior Pattern.

The Negative Behavior Pattern

I am sure none of us wants our worst behavior to be the basis of how we are perceived and treated. We all know rationally that people are more than just the negative acts the commit. Yet, we see many cases in which Person A does something Person B considers especially deplorable, and the positive things Person A has done, is doing, and will do in the future are ignored. The bad behavior becomes a Dot obscuring the Circle. Let's look at a brief example.

Negative Behavior Example
For six years, Nancy has worked at a company called New Technologies (NuTech). Alex, her boss, has consistently given her

positive job performance evaluations. Last week, Alex gave Nancy a complicated task assignment involving a long-time major client, saying the task had to be completed in two days. Nancy immediately said the job required at least a week, and asked Alex to assign another worker to help. It was the first time Nancy had ever made such a request. Alex refused, saying he gave the assignment to Nancy because her excellent work record showed she was the best person for the job. "Get it done," was his final comment.

The other workers at NuTech expressed their firm opinion that nobody, not even the skilled and diligent Nancy, could complete the assignment in two days. Their prediction proved correct. Although Nancy worked late into the night, there was no way she could complete the task by the deadline. The client immediately took its business to a rival company.

The president of NuTech, angry the client had been lost, blamed both Alex and Nancy and told Alex to "fix the problem". Alex called Nancy into his office and fired her on the spot. NuTech lost an excellent worker, the other employees lost respect for Alex, and the effectiveness of the company suffered.

Obviously, Alex allowed Nancy's failure to meet the deadline to become a Dot. The overall situation was ignored. So let's help Alex "broaden his picture" by using the Circle & Dot LifeSkill.

What are the other components in the Circle, the broader context, besides Nancy not being able to meet the deadline? Here are a few of the most important components.

(1) Nancy's excellent record for six years.

(2) A clear assessment of whether or not any one person could complete the task in two days.

(3) Why the client took its business to a rival company. Could there be reasons other than this one assignment not being completed by the deadline?

(4) The effects firing Nancy would have on the morale of the other workers and on the effectiveness of Alex's leadership.

Alex never considered these components of the overall situation. He allowed one act--- Nancy's "worst behavior" in not meeting the deadline---to obscure the bigger picture. If he had used LifeSkill #1, he and Nancy could have found more effective ways to deal with the situation.

When a Negative Behavior Dot Is Considered To Be of Paramount Importance

As you will remember, Step 6 in the Circle & Dot LifeSkill focuses on the relative importance of a Dot to the overall situation. As we all know, there are cases in which a particular negative act is considered by a person, group or system to be of such great importance that it determines decisions. A relationship is ended because of that one act, an interaction is ruined, or, yes, a person is fired.

Every person, of course, has a right to decide how important a particular behavior is to him or her. *But that decision needs to be based on a comprehensive view of the person committing the behavior and the overall situation.* And that's what using LifeSkill #1 can help us do. Several questions are important to consider.

Is that particular behavior really worth ending a relationship? Are there enough other positive things in the relationship to move forward even though that behavior should never have been done and perhaps can never be completely "forgiven"?

Has a particular type of behavior become a pattern, or was it just a one-time occurrence?

Are there reasons for the behavior that have not been considered? Does discovering some of those reasons make the behavior more understandable and less "severe" within the overall relationship or interaction?

Planning

Many books have been written on "planning", so I will focus only on how this LifeSkill can apply. The "Planning Circle" contains many components, including who takes part in the planning, what the goals are, what resources are needed and how to get them, who the beneficiaries of the plan are, who does what by when, the desired outcomes, and other considerations. If we do not look at all these critical components, our planning will not be effective.

The Circle & Dot LifeSkill can help enrich planning in several ways. I will comment on three of the most crucial.

Focusing on Process, not Only on Outcomes

Effective outcomes emerge from effective Process. The shape and strength of the outcomes are determined by a process pathway composed of many interconnected steps. Yet, planning often puts much more emphasis on desired outcomes than on Process, turning certain goals and certain outcomes into "Dots". Outcomes are important, of course, but their ultimate success will be greatly enhanced by an effective Process.

The Circle & Dot LifeSkill serves as a beginning step in building a strong process pathway.

Let's look at some of the important components in the "Planning Circle".

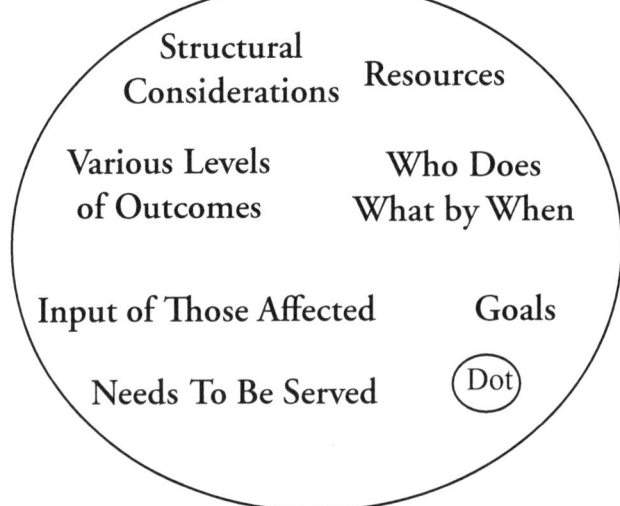

The Planning Circle

The broader context of any planning endeavor includes many components.

• "All-party Connectors" are things that link together the planners, the beneficiaries, the resource providers, the stakeholders, and other individuals or groups who will be affected by the plans. The all-party connectors usually include shared needs as a major link.

• Needs: What needs is the plan designed to serve?
• Goals: Short-term and long-term goals
• Resources needed and how to get them.
• Input in the planning process from the people or groups who will be most affected.
• Planning for various outcome levels
• Who Does What by When
• Structural Considerations: Awareness of the social, cultural, economic, political, etc. structures/systems in which the plan must operate, and what structures, if any, need to be changed in order for the plan to be successful. Do the planners have the influence and power to bring about those changes? If not, the planning must adjust accordingly.
• On-going assessment and flexibility to make improvements based on the assessment.

(NOTE: You will notice the "Dot" is left blank in the graphic. Comments on some of the more prevalent Dots that occur in planning will be offered later.)

I would like to focus now on two of the components in the planning process that are often ignored or given inadequate attention.

Preparing for Various Outcomes (the "What-If" Planning Strategy)

The "What-If Step" of planning looks at the broader context, the Circle, and realizes there are at least three levels of possible outcomes:

<u>Top Level</u> (the best possible outcomes result)

<u>Middle Level</u> (some parts of the plan turn out as hoped, some do not)

<u>Low Level</u> (most things do not turn out as planned and a lot of redesigning needs to occur)

Many planning endeavors prepare only for Top Level outcomes. But "What If" those most desired outcomes might not result? Has anything been built into the plans to deal with the possibility of Middle Level or Low Level outcomes? If not, the planning group and the plan itself may not be able to respond and adjust effectively.

Including the Input of Those Who Will Be Affected by the Plans

From the very beginning of the planning process, those who will be most affected by the plan need to be significant members of the planning group. They are closest to the actual situation, and their perspectives on what is needed and what will work and not work are crucial to the success of the plan. They usually point out parts of the broader situation the other members of the planning group may not be considering.

Furthermore, if those people most affected are an integral part of the planning process, their belief in and commitment to the eventual plan will be enhanced. Without that commitment, they will be less likely to do their part in making the plan work effectively. (NOTE: Including the input of people and groups whose voices are usually ignored in other aspects of life is especially important.)

Here is a real-life example of what can happen if the elements of LifeSkill #1 are not applied to the planning process.

Planning Example: The Village Project

A large international development organization wanted to initiate a project in a country beset with ethnic conflict and numerous other problems. The organization chose a particular village for the project because it offered the best chance of success. The two ethnic groups living in the village had somehow managed to resolve their conflicts peacefully for several centuries, which was in stark contrast to the numerous wars fought by the same ethnic groups in other parts of the region.

The organization sent two representatives to the village to determine what the project should be. Following their usual pattern, the representatives talked only to the village leaders, which in this case was the Headman and two elders. The other citizens of the village were not consulted.

The representatives immediately noticed that the only water supply system consisted of the women of the village walking two miles to the river every morning. They collected water and carried it back to the village in large urns balanced on their heads. Believing that was an inefficient way to get water, the organization decided to develop a project that piped water from the river. The Headman and the two elders liked the idea, partly because they would have control over how the water would be distributed among the villagers.

After the project had been operating for three months, uncharacteristic conflicts began popping up throughout the village. That's when the organization requested my services as a consultant. The director said, "What's wrong with these villagers? We gave them a great project, and now they are fighting against each other for the first time in centuries!"

When I met with the organization, the first thing I did was draw the Circle & Dot diagram and explain what it represented. Here is an abbreviated rendition of the initial conversation that followed. (I am "DW", the organization is "ORG".)

DW: What are some things in the Circle, the Broader Context, you considered when you were deciding on a project?
ORG: We immediately saw the inefficient water supply method they were using. The choice of a project was easy.
DW: What else about the village life did you consider? Let's put some of them in the Circle.
ORG: (somewhat baffled) We saw a major problem and fixed it. That's what we do in all our projects around the world.
DW: In deciding on and planning the piped water project, who had input?

Life in the Quality Lane

ORG: Our experts from headquarters, of course, and the Headman and elders.

DW: Let's keep looking at the Circle. What other parts of village life are affected by the water project? Did you consider any of those in your decision and your planning?

ORG: (a bit frustrated) Look. We saw a problem and we fixed it. But now we're concerned all of these new conflicts are hurting our project.

(I filled in the "Dot" with "Water Project".)

DW: I have a suggestion. Spend the next week listening to villagers other than the Headman and two elders. See if they can give you insight into some of the other issues involved, and put those things in the Circle.

The representatives of the organization spent the next week listening to the villagers and filling in the Circle. One of the components the organization learned about was a highly functional tradition that had proven effective for centuries.

The walk to the river every morning was understood and accepted by all the villagers as the time the women performed their traditional conflict resolution role in the society. Away from the conflict-producing manipulations of the men in the village, the women used the walk to the river to sort out the conflicts of village life.

By ignoring the Broader Context and fixating only on piping water to the village, the organization had completely missed this vital component of the situation. *Even though bringing water to the village more efficiently was accomplished, it affected and was affected by other important issues of the overall situation.*

To their credit, the leaders of the organization expanded their project. They listened to the suggestions of the villagers and ended up adding a Meeting House as a companion project. The House was used solely by the women of the village for a certain time each day so they could have a private place to carry on their traditional role as the "problem-solvers and conflict resolution experts" of the village. The Headman, elders, and other men in the village readily accepted the arrangement because they, too, suffered from the conflicts that had emerged since the project began.

Keeping the Circle & Dot image ever-present in our minds empowers us to understand situations more comprehensively and to improve our effectiveness in all we do. To close our chapter on LifeSkill #1, Focus on the Broader Context, a final graphic (next page) shows some

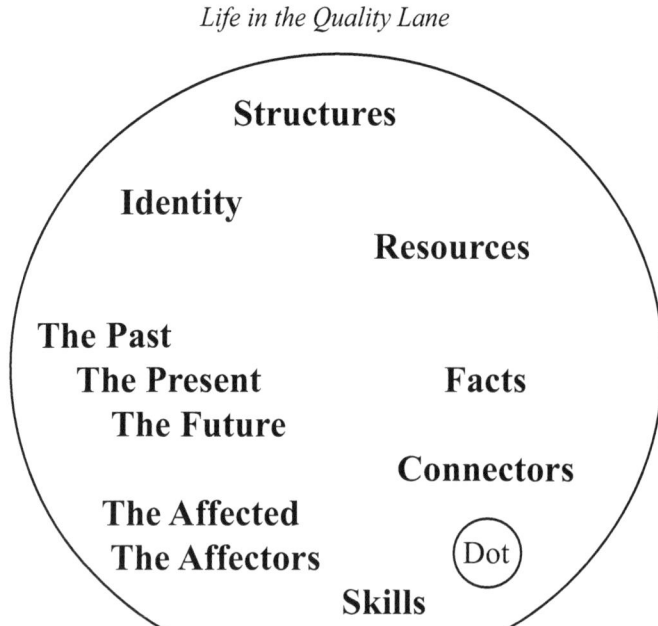

Regardless of the specific situation, the components included in the Circle above will always be inportant parts of the Broader Context. Depending on the situation, some will be more important than others, but all need to be considered.

Chapter 2

LifeSkill #2: Focus on Connections

We are connected one to the other
by needs and hopes that transcend
infant groupings so recently spawned
by divisive minds in this human cradle
from which we've still not emerged
with gentle strength, so we reach
for dominance and reach for advantage
to feel we deserve a higher place than someone else....
but we are connected, one to the other,
with more in common than we want to see,
for I need you and you need me,
connected as we are in this cradle bed,
the same umbilical feeds us all,
when you draw breath my lungs expand,
when I fall down your body aches.....
we are connected the one to the whole,
woven as art in search of a frame,
yet we seem to dwell
on the torn interruptions
ignoring the truth
that we are connected.

(From the poetry collection
So Far To Go When We Get There
by Dudley Weeks)

"Connectors" link people together constructively even though there are things that divide them. In any interaction, any situation, connectors are a key component of the Broader Context, the Circle. They may be in the form of shared needs, goals, beliefs, aspects of identity, interests, unwanted outcomes, and a host of other linkages with another person or group.

Identifying connectors at an early point in an interaction not only helps us realize we have positive linkages to build upon, it also helps us deal more effectively with what divides us. Yet, when we have differences with others, when we compete with others, and especially when we have strong conflicts with others, some people tend to ignore the potentially constructive connections they still have with those people and groups.

I find it both perplexing and sad that human beings and human society often seem more adept at focusing on things that divide us, rather than looking for and utilizing the many things that "connect" us constructively.

Perhaps one reason for this pattern is our infancy as a social species, that we are still searching for who we are and want to become. In trying to get a secure sense of Self, we mistakenly fixate on how we are different from others in the hope our own Self Identity will then be clarified.

Perhaps another reason is that in our desire to justify our own opinions and our particular ways of doing things, we try to find "lesser" in others. We create the convenient, self-serving illusion that we are "good" or "right" because they are "bad" or "wrong".

Or it could be that in our appreciation of Diversity, which we have learned is a positive aspect of human society, we forget it is also important to focus on and strengthen all those important things we have in common.

Whatever the reasons, when we ignore "connections" we weaken ourselves, our relationships, our interactions, and our societies. We become less effective and perform with less quality. Connections are not only parts of the Broader Context (the Circle) of any situation, they are also vital building blocks for bringing quality to our interactions, building effective personal and professional relationships, dealing well with conflicts, and developing cooperation.

Although there are many kinds of connectors, I will focus on five that have consistently proven to be helpful in living our lives with greater effectiveness and quality. We touched on some of these in Chapter 1.

1. Connectors Linking Components of the Broader Context

If we refer back to the Circle & Dot graphic on the last page of Chapter 1, we see "Connectors" is one of the components in the Circle. However, it is important to note that all of the components have some kind of connection with each other. How we deal with each has an effect on the others.

To review, one of the most significant connections is the one linking the Dot to the Broader Context. Fixating on a Dot affects and is affected by the other components in the Circle. Some of the other components can help us deal with the Dot, and if we put the Dot in its proper perspective as just one of the many components of a situation, we can move forward more effectively.

2. Identity Connectors

As discussed earlier, a person's "total" identity is part of the Broader Context of any interaction, any relationship. In other words, every person has many aspects to her or his identity. Some of those aspects, such as gender, race, ethnicity, family, physical size, and original nationality and culture are the result of birth. Other identity aspects are, eventually, matters of choice, such as religion, professions, beliefs on issues, the values we hold, and our behavior patterns, to mention only a few.

As we all know, many relationships are based on aspects of identity that "connect" people (similar interests, jobs, belief systems, etc.). Yet, our experiences show us that having relationships with people who are different than we are can help us grow as complete people. Sadly, we often let those differences cause an "I versus you" and "us versus them" mentality, tempting us to divide ourselves from people who are different. The *connectors* that still exist are ignored, and damaging and seemingly intractable conflict is often the result.

We should be familiar with the problems created when a person is perceived only in terms of race, gender, ethnicity, nationality, religion, and any other single identity component. Every day, we see the conflicts such narrow thinking produces. We will explore this phenomenon in greater depth later, but for now we will look at several examples of Identity Connectors. As we do, I hope you will be thinking of a person or group with whom you would normally assume no connections exist, and find one or two.

Example A: The Mothers

I was conducting a training workshop in a country long beset with a conflict partially based on religion. A woman I'll call Eva was attending the workshop. One evening after the workshop, Eva, her sister (whose husband had recently died), and her sister's two daughters were walking on a city street when a car bomb exploded. In the wrong place at the wrong time, the sister and one of her daughters were accidentally killed.

Eva, unmarried and living alone, suddenly became a surrogate "mother" as she adopted her late sister's surviving daughter. Deeply affected by the continuing, senseless violence in the society, Eva committed herself to applying the LifeSkill, "Focus on Connections". She courageously decided to take action. During the next week, she crossed the dividing line between the two warring religious groups and began knocking on the doors of homes in which the "enemy" lived. When the door was answered, she asked, "Is there a mother in the house?" <u>She was taking her new identity as a mother and trying to connect with the "mother" aspect of identity within the other conflict group</u>.

Some people slammed the door in her face, but some responded positively. She organized a meeting of mothers from both conflict groups, and soon a community organization of mothers from both religious groups was created. That organization became a powerful force for conflict resolution and reconciliation in the society. Aspects of the conflict were still there, but acting on at least one connector in the midst of the things that divided the two groups provided a foundation on which to deal with the conflict more effectively.

Example B: The Youth Center

Several years ago, I did some volunteer work at the only Youth Center in a racially divided community. Segregated neighborhoods, churches, and other institutions existed throughout the community, and acts of violence occurred several times each month, usually involving youth gangs based on race.

The Center had recently opened, and the director was searching for ways to make the Center effective. He felt the only way to avoid having the Center become just one more battleground was to have a schedule based on race. One race would use the Center on Monday,

Wednesday and Friday, and the other race on Tuesday, Thursday and Saturday. In my discussions with him, I asked what I felt were two key questions.

The first question was, "What messages do you think such a plan sends to the youth?"

After some thought, he replied, "Well, I guess it might be seen as defining the youth only by their race. And it could send the message that the Center thinks the two races can't interact cooperatively and have to be separated."

My next question was, "What are some things connecting the youth, things that have nothing to do with race?"

After some discussion, he wisely suggested we ask the youth that question. We did, and the youth of both races identified several "connectors". They all wanted computer training, dance activities, athletic teams, and academic tutoring. Race had nothing to do with those connectors. Within a month, the Center was running daily programs based on the connectors the youth of both races had identified. Race became less and less important in how the youth perceived themselves and each other.

Example C: An Exercise To Promote "Identity Connectors"

In many of the LifeSkills workshops I conduct, I find that if a portion of the training focuses on Identity Connectors, other skills such as Conflict Resolution, Leadership, Cooperative Planning, Organizational Development, and Managing Effective Change will be enhanced. However, one does not have to be a professional trainer to suggest and implement creative exercises that can assist the discovery of Identity Connectors. Here is one exercise I have developed and utilize frequently, and many teachers, community workers, and organizations are also using the exercise.

<u>First,</u> pairs are formed by putting together two people who are different in age, or gender, or race, or ethnicity, or religion, or political affiliation, or socio-economic group, or nationality, or profession, or views on a contentious issue, etc.

<u>Second</u>, the paired partners share with each other five Self-identity components that are important in her/his perception of the Self. Values are often mentioned, or hobbies, or beliefs, or favorite activities, whatever each person feels is an important part of who she or he is.

<u>Third</u>, the partners look for an Identity Connector among the Self-identity components they described to each other.

Fourth, the partners then use that Identity Connector as the foundation on which they will design the broad outlines of a community project that will benefit both partners and their respective groups in the community.

This exercise has resulted in numerous peacebuilding and community development projects. For example, the Identity Connector found by two partners of different ethnic and religious backgrounds was music. Both played a musical instrument, one had even been a member of a musical group, and both saw the love of music as an important part of their Self Identity. Using music as their connector, the two partners then designed a community project in which a mixed-ethnic musical group would be organized to present concerts in both sections of the community that had long been divided into conflicting ethnic/religious groupings.

In spite of conflicts between the ethnic groups, the mixed-ethnic music group gave the community a practical example of how working with each other, rather than always working against each other, was both possible and mutually beneficial. Other projects followed after the "breakthrough" music group had proven cooperation was possible.

Although this particular example is taken from a war zone during very tense times, the lesson applies to any relationship, family, community, organization, business, or situation. Finding and developing Identity Connectors, even in the midst of conflicts, can be extremely helpful. Building on those Identity Connectors is greatly enhanced through the use of the other LifeSkills we will discuss in subsequent chapters.

3. Shared Needs Connectors

Shared Needs are specific needs all the parties involved in a relationship, interaction, or situation have in common. Shared Needs exist in most every situation, even those in which serious disagreements also exist. When we identify Shared Needs, they become "building blocks" on which partnership action can be developed. They can help people move beyond impasse and the notion "there is nothing we agree on".

Let's get a glimpse of how valuable Shared Needs connectors can be when recognized and utilized, and how ignoring them can lead to problems.

Example D: Mina, Stan, and the Children

Mina and Stan, married for twelve years and the parents of two children whom they loved deeply, decided to get a divorce. For various reasons, they had steadily grown apart, both feeling increasingly unfulfilled in the relationship.

The divorce process became very nasty. Fights over possessions, bank accounts, and who was more at fault for ruining the marriage dominated the situation. The children, a boy and a girl, heard and watched it all with increasing sadness and confusion. They wondered if they had done something wrong to make their parents fight and want to split up. The children began to take sides in the battle, and felt their own previously strong relationship with each other was also falling apart.

The way the divorce was handled damaged everybody. Both Mina and Stan had become obsessed with the things that divided them. Even the children became pawns in the battle, and the war over custody was brutal. Both children ended up spending a lot of time with a psychologist for the three years following the divorce.

To be sure, Mina and Stan had serious divisions. But they also had Shared Need connections, a major one being the need to make sure the psychological welfare of the children would not be damaged by the divorce. Another need both Mina and Stan shared was to have the divorce handled in a way that would not damage their continuing friendships in the neighborhood and larger community. If they had focused on those and other Shared Needs, they would have dealt with the divorce in a much more constructive manner.

As you no doubt recognize, both Stan and Mina focused on certain "Dots" based on material desires and on "winning" in the divorce battle. The psychological welfare of the children, a major Shared Need connecting all the family members, was obscured by the fixation on the Dots. Recognizing that Shared Need connector could have helped Mina and Stan move beyond their respective Dots.

4. Value-Behavior Connectors

We will be more effective people and perform with higher quality if there is consistency between our values and our behavior, if our behavior expresses the values we hold dear. To hold and espouse certain values, then to behave contrary to those values, lessens both our self-respect and the respect others have of us. Furthermore, <u>dis</u>connecting one's values and behavior creates confusion and conflict in relationships and interactions.

I have learned from my own mistakes that people are better able to change certain behavior patterns they need to change if they recognize the current behavior is not expressing, or is even contradicting, one of their important values. When they make the change, they realize even more the importance of the value-behavior connection because they begin to feel better about themselves and feel more Self-secure, and the quality of their relationships, interactions, and personal and professional endeavors improves.

Let's look at some examples of Values-Behavior Connectors.

Example E: Bev and Her Daughter

A friend of mine (I'll call her Bev) who is a fairly successful stage actress talked to me about her relationship with her daughter, who was just graduating from high school. Three years earlier, the husband/father had died in an auto accident, and the adjustment for both Bev and her daughter had been difficult. Bev felt they had managed life fairly well, and the typical "terrible teens" so many parents face had not been a major problem.

When Bev called me, she expressed shock that problems were now appearing in her relationship with her daughter. "She even called me a hypocrite last night," Bev told me. "That hurt. I feel something churning inside me, and I don't know what it is."

Being an actress, she gave the "churning" comment a lot of dramatic emphasis, but I could tell she was sincere. Something was eating away at her.

In the course of our conversation, I suggested she confront the question, "Am I connecting my behavior to my values?", and I gave her an example from my own life of when my behavior had contradicted one of my important values. Bev took the question seriously and made an important discovery.

She had always placed high value on the right of young people to make their own choices about "what I want to be when I grow up". As she considered the question "Am I connecting my behavior to my values?", she realized she was violating that value by fiercely opposing her daughter's determination to become an actress.

When I asked her reasons, Bev said, "The acting field is full of negative temptations.... her failing miserably is likely, given the fierce competition for roles....and she is determined to move from New York to Los Angeles to pursue a movie career. I know what you're thinking. I left home and moved to New York when I was 17, but it's a different world now."

"This 'churning' sensation," I asked, "what do you think it comes from?"

"Well, now that I ask the question you suggested, I guess the churning comes from realizing that my actions are violating my strong belief that young people have the right to make their own choices. She hasn't accused me of that, but it's probably true. And it's making me feel like I really may be a hypocrite, and it's hurting our relationship. She says I give her confusing messages."

"So what are you going to do about it?" I asked.

What Bev did was to take her daughter on a camping trip, an activity they both greatly enjoyed (an "enjoyable activity connector", we might call it). On the trip, Mom went through her worries about movie careers, the daughter asked for advice, Mom restored the value-behavior connection by supporting the daughter's firm decision to become an actress, and the daughter decided to start pursuing her acting career in New York and consider Hollywood later. (Here's a rather irrelevant postscript, perhaps of interest only to soap opera lovers. The daughter got her first acting role on a soap four months later.)

Example F: South Africa

South Africa is a fascinating society. I have great admiration for the people of all races who did what most of the world felt was impossible: make fundamental, comprehensive change through peaceful means. I have had the honor and good fortune to work with those people in their efforts. I learned a lot from their courage, wisdom, and commitment.

Part of my work was with the youth of all races. As with many youth world-wide, one of the values held by the young people in South Africa was, and still is, "mattering". They want to matter, to have their lives be of significance. During the Apartheid system of racial separation, "mattering" often involved using violent behavior to be "powerful" because, as many youth told me, "When I hit or kill someone, there's a clear and immediate effect. I feel powerful.".

Decades of violence had contributed to the misperception that to be powerful, to "matter", involves using violence successfully. If South Africa was to build a strong, effective society, that misperception had to change. *The value of "mattering", of being "powerful", of being "significant", needed to find behavior that would express that value* **constructively** .

Many youth responded magnificently to alternative behavior opportunities. They found constructive, nonviolent ways to matter and be powerful. They connected their values and behavior.

Thousands of youth became trainers in conflict resolution. They also developed and implemented multi-racial projects in communities, organizations, churches, schools and businesses.

Another value and goal many South Africans held strongly---their nation being respected internationally---was also served by their changed behavior in relationships, communities, organizations, institutions, businesses, schools, churches, and other sectors of the society.

South Africa has embarked on the long and difficult road of peaceful societal transformation. There will be stumbles along the way, as is true with any society. But they are proving that any person, any group, any society that values peace and mutually beneficial relationships must make their behavior consistent with those values. They must build and sustain the Value-Behavior Connection.

Three Additional Values-Behavior Connections
- **Goals and Ethics**. If a goal is achieved through unethical behavior, three results usually occur. (1) Additional unethical behavior is used to protect the goal after it is achieved. Once unethical behavior is considered acceptable, it becomes a pattern. (2) The quality of the goal is diminished. (3) Support for the achieved goal lessens.

Many examples exist at both micro and macro levels, one macro example being Economic Profit and Ethics. A lack of ethics is often one of the major contributors to economic crises.
- **Process and Outcome**. *Effective outcomes emerge from effective Process.* Furthermore, a flawed process produces a flawed outcome. Yet, many people are so goal-oriented they give little attention to Process.
- **Freedom and Responsibility**. Without responsibility, "freedom" can become a license for self-serving action, exploiting others, and doing whatever one pleases.

5. The Most Fundamental Connection

Any discussion of connectors needs to include the most fundamental of all: the connection humans have with the Earth's ecosystem. We are but one, interrelated part of the Earth system. Humans are not superior to the ecosystem, nor are we exempt from the Principles essential for the survival and positive development of all organisms, including what I term "social organisms" (relationships, interactions, organizations, communities, nations, and the global human society).

As we all know, ignoring this connection can produce devastating environmental problems that negatively affect the entire ecosystem, including humans. But that is only one of the results. *Once we become accustomed to ignoring connections in one aspect of life, especially in this most fundamental of all aspects, we are far more likely to ignore many of the other vital connections that fill our lives.*

Perhaps a personal experience from my childhood can provide a vivid picture of this most fundamental connection. I grew up in a part of the country where racism, sexism, ageism, and opposition to anything other than the dominant patterns were deeply entrenched. I did not feel at home with those attitudes, behaviors and structures. I spent many evenings lying on my back outside looking at the stars and corridors among the stars. I wished wise creatures from space would explain to me why I was supposed to follow the dominant patterns I felt were obstructing the development of our positive potential.

And then one starry night when I was five, I had a profound experience. *I imagined roots growing from my body down into the Earth.* I felt at home, I felt *connected.* A simple yet powerful realization hit me. All of humanity can learn from the Earth about how diverse parts, each with its special contributions, can work together....for the benefit of each other and the Whole.

"Focus on Connections" is a powerful LifeSkill. It can help us build effective relationships, make interactions constructive, deal with conflict, and strengthen our organizations, businesses and societies.

We now move to an exploration of LifeSkill #3: Secure I, Secure Other, Secure We.

Chapter 3

LifeSkill #3: Develop Secure Self, Secure Other, Secure We

I am,
You are,
each stronger
when we feel secure
within the Self.

And if there is
to be a We,
the I and You
will each gain strength
by helping the other
remain secure
within ourselves
and within the We.

Applying the first two LifeSkills helps us understand the broader context of a situation, and to identify constructive Connectors. Building on that solid foundation, we are ready to explore the additional LifeSkills that help empower us to be effective in all we do. The next one is Develop Secure Self, Secure Other, Secure We.

Rather than beginning our discussion by consulting a dictionary definition of "secure", I would like to consult you. First, I will ask you a question and request you give some thought to your responses before we move on. Here is the question.

When do you feel secure?

(Please give the question some thought.)

Now that you have responded to the question, I invite you to do the next task in the exercise. Please finish the following sentence with as many responses as you choose to offer. (Some may be similar to your responses to the first question.)

In my relationships and interactions, I feel secure when.........

Although the responses generated by this little exercise will vary from person to person, I suggest there are some essential components that apply to all of us, components that are integral parts of what being "secure" means....as individuals, and as participants in any relationship and interaction.

Key Components of Being Secure
The Secure SELF

Feeling secure within oneself adds to the quality of life and helps a person be effective. There are many ingredients that constitute a Secure Self. I will focus on only a few.

I am secure within myself when.......

- I understand I am more than any single part of my total identity.

- I have a clear understanding of the most important attitudes, ethics, and values I want to guide my life, and I try to make my behavior express those attitudes, ethics, and values.

- I am aware of the Broader Context of situations, and I am careful not to fixate on any one component to the detriment of everything else.

- I welcome and embrace diversity, I do not fear it. People have a right to be different, and if I am secure within myself, I do not feel a need to force others to adopt my opinions, beliefs, preferences, etc.
- I know and admit my limitations and mistakes, and I am open to self- improvement.
- I focus on what I am doing, rather than spending time and energy wishing I were somewhere else, doing something else.
- I focus on things that are within my power to influence and accomplish, things I can do, yet I am also committed to the development of my potential so that I might become capable of turning a "can't do" into a "can do".
- I am not afraid of change, and if I believe change is needed, I try to suggest improved alternatives rather than just criticizing and complaining about the way things are at present.

As highly socialized creatures, we spend an enormous amount of time and energy participating in relationships and interactions with other people and groups. *Having a Secure Self helps us conduct our relationships and interactions with greater quality, more confidence, more clarity, and more effectiveness.*

If the people we are interacting with also feel secure within themselves and in their dealings with us, even more worthwhile possibilities can be developed. Linking the Secure Self and the Secure Other together, we need to focus on an important Principle:

The effectiveness of any relationship, any interaction, will be enhanced if all parties feel secure in their dealings with each other. We have the power to help other people and groups feel secure in their interactions with us. If they feel secure, it helps us feel secure, and if we feel secure, it helps them feel secure.

Even though these principles have been proven time and time again, we often find ourselves facing a pattern that has become far too prevalent. Many people and groups, especially in conflict situations, choose to believe and promote the myth, "I will be more secure if I make you feel insecure." We must not let that myth rule us. For in reality, *the more insecure the other party feels, the more likely it is that destructive and unpredictable behavior will occur.* Damage to both parties usually results.

Now, let's explore The Secure Other.

The Secure **OTHER**

In our relationships and interactions, the Secure Other involves two major categories of feeling "secure".

- <u>How secure the other party feels within herself or himself</u> (that person's Secure Self).

Some people we interact with are already secure within themselves, some are not. We may have some influence, but we cannot determine how secure anyone else feels as a person. That is ultimately up to that person.

- <u>How secure the other party feels in a relationship or interaction with us.</u>

We have much more influence on how secure other people feel in whatever relationship or interaction we share with them.

I believe I have a responsibility to help people feel secure in their relationships and interactions with me, including when we are involved in conflict situations.

Among the many things we can do to help build that feeling of security, here are a few suggestions that consistently prove dependable. Not surprisingly, some are the same or similar to the steps involved in developing a secure Self.

Helping Others Feel Secure in Their Dealings with Us

1. *Perceive and treat others in their <u>totality</u>.*

When we perceive and treat others based on only one aspect of their Identity, they feel less secure in their dealings with us because they are not being accepted as who they really are in their totality. The same is true of behavior. If we perceive others based only on a particular behavior we find to be deplorable, we are being short-sighted. Every person is more than just his or her worst behavior.

2. *Actively invite others to offer their opinions, listen attentively, and perceive those opinions as contributions to mutual discovery and growth.*

Most people seem to appreciate being invited to express their opinions, even if they decline to do so. People tend to feel secure if we (a) invite their opinions <u>before</u> giving our own; (b) let them express opinions without interrupting; (c) look for points of agreement with our own opinions first; and (d) treat the points of disagreement as opportunities for mutual discovery and growth.

3. *Invite and promote the participation of others.*

This is especially important in situations where certain people are in positions or roles that make it easy, and sometimes expected, to exclude their participation. Three examples are:

(a) involving children in family decisions
(b) having a system through which employees can regularly offer suggestions for improving the workplace

(c) inviting and developing <u>partnership</u> conflict resolution with someone involved in a conflict with us.

4. *Focus on positive connections we have with others, not just on things that divide us.*

5. *Be attentive to other people's emotional needs, rather than treating them as a nuisance, or burden to bear, or a trick to gain sympathy and advantage.*

Understanding why others feel as they do is important. Judging them is not helpful, nor is trying to play the role of an amateur psychiatrist. Sometimes listening is enough, sometimes giving them space is best, and sometimes suggesting a specific <u>activity</u> that directs their emotional energy in constructive or fun activities can be helpful.

6. *Communicate clearly. Unclear communication leaves people confused and can lead to their feeling insecure.*

A few of the many examples include (a) confusing job descriptions at the workplace; (b) parents giving unclear instructions to children; (c) vague instruction manuals for how to assemble or use products; (d) claiming to believe in a value but not living it; (e) not clarifying perceptions; and (f) not differentiating between needs and desires, or assumptions and facts.

7. *Do not use overt or covert threats.*

In international relations, the threats are usually overt. In personal relationships, they are often covert, such as, "If you really loved me, you would....."

8. *Try to limit our own rigid expectations.*

We can have hopes, but once we start to expect others to think and behave as we want them to, we create a breeding ground for insecurity. The more times they fail to meet those rigid expectations, the less secure they feel in the relationship and the less secure the overall relationship becomes.

9. *Build "positive" trust.*

Positive trust helps build an effective and secure Self, secure Other, and secure We. "Positive" trust is based on three vital principles.

One, we need to communicate clearly what each party needs from the other in order to be able to trust. Both people will feel encouraged to be honest about their capabilities in fulfilling that trust, and the chances that either will be hit with an unexpected "You betrayed my trust!" outburst will be reduced. An honest discussion of "boundaries" can also be important.

Two, we need to realize that "trusting" and "living up to expectations" are not synonymous. Some people act as though they feel their <u>expectations</u> of someone else must be met in order for trust to exist. Often, the other person is not even aware of what was expected. When the "I can't trust you" statement is issued after the uncommunicated expectation goes unmet, developing a "positive" trust becomes more difficult.

Three, most people want to be trusted, and here is a sampling of things we can do to gain the trust of others.

(a) Make our behavior consistent with those values and priorities we espouse.

(b) Consistently say what we mean and mean what we say.

(c) Avoid promising what we cannot do or do not intend to do.

(d) Be as sincerely interested in what someone else needs are as we are in what we need.

(e) Clarify our perceptions and what they are based on.

(f) Clearly express our own needs and hopes, rather than assuming they should be obvious.

Attaining a Secure Self and a Secure Other adds significantly to the development of a Secure We. Thus, most of the suggestions already offered in this chapter also apply to this next section. We will look now at a few additional steps involved in developing a Secure We.

The Secure WE

- <u>Invite "partnership"</u> from the very beginning of an interaction, even if the other party is acting as though an adversarial atmosphere is the only one possible. (The statement, "I want to work with you, not against you" is a basic beginning point in inviting partnership.)

- Develop *Power-WITH* (TM). "Power-WITH" is a term I coined in previous writings to describe a kind of power directly opposite to the competition for "power-over" so often utilized in interactions. (NOTE: See LifeSkill #5, in Chapter Five, for a more thorough discussion of Power-WITH.)

- Working for <u>mutual</u> benefits goes hand in hand with a Secure We.

- A Secure We is made more possible when we perceive <u>disagreements and conflicts</u> not as inherently negative but as conditions through which needs, perceptions, feelings, and action steps can be clarified. Conflicts can even lead to an improvement in relationships and interactions if we understand and utilize the LifeSkills discussed in this book.

I am sure you have thought of many examples from your own experiences demonstrating the importance of LifeSkill #3, Develop Secure Self, Secure Other, Secure We. I would like to end the chapter with a final example. Although it is taken from the international arena, it also applies to any intense relationship or interaction in which "feeling secure" is difficult to attain.

Closing Example

Based on my work in the Middle East, I will present a portion of one of the actual meetings I have had with many Israelis and many Palestinians. In the dialogue format below, I am referred to as "D", and "I/P" refers to both the Israelis and Palestinians since their responses to my questions are almost always identical.

D: What are your primary needs?
I/P: One primary need is to feel secure.
D: Can you describe what feeling 'secure' means?
I/P: Well, for one thing, not being under constant attack or the threat of attack.
D: Can you think of what would help the possible attackers choose NOT to attack?
I/P: (a traditional international relations response) They won't attack if they know we can defeat them....or if we attack first and cripple them so much they won't be able to attack us. We need to have enough weapons, and enough will, to protect ourselves.
D: How much weaponry will you need to accumulate, and how much of your budget will need to be spent on the military and police in order to have 'enough'?
I/P: Whatever it takes.
D: Those times you have attacked first.....what were the reasons?
I/P: We felt threatened and insecure because we are confronted by hostile enemies...and we know they want to destroy us. So we preempt that possibility by attacking them before they can attack us.
D: Let me see if I understand. I hear you saying that feeling insecure is one of the things that has led to your conducting preemptive strikes? Is that what you mean?
I/P: Yes. Feeling constantly threatened makes anybody feel insecure.

	The kind of relationship we have with them makes us feel insecure. We can't trust them.
D:	Do you think they feel the same way about the relationship?
I/P:	Probably.
D;	Has attacking each other made either of you feel more secure?
I/P:	(pause) I guess not. But we don't have a choice.
D:	If feeling insecure is one of the reasons for attacking each other, would removing some of the insecurity in the relationship make attacks less likely?"
I/P:	Well….I suppose that does makes sense. But…..
D:	I would like to invite you to think of one step, however small, that could help make them feel more secure in their relationship with you. I'll ask them to do the same when I meet with them. We now turn to LifeSkill #4: *Clarify*.

Chapter 4

LifeSkill #4: Clarify

Without clarity
we cannot discern
reality from illusion,
ennui from concern,
    dusk from dawn
    nights from days,
    what's up or down
    or maybe sideways,
        who I am
        and who I'm not,
        who you are
        and who you're not,
            what steps to take
            in making a plan,
            or find solid ground
            instead of deadly quicksand.

Clarification is one of life's most essential skills. If we fail to clarify, we run the risk of basing our thoughts and actions on incorrect information, faulty assumptions, and misleading presumptions, all of which obstruct our ability to be relevant and effective. The quality of our lives suffers.

Although "Clarify" is one of the most obvious of the LifeSkills, it is often ignored or done inadequately. Why? Here are a few possible explanations.

(a) Our formal and informal education does not put enough emphasis on the importance of clarification, or on identifying and teaching practical clarification skills.

(b) Some people think clarification takes too much time and effort, so they charge ahead on unclarified ground. In actuality, more time and energy is required to repair the effects of not clarifying than if clarification had been done from the very beginning.

(c) Relying on unfounded rumors and assumptions is a tempting yet inadequate substitute for effective clarification.

(d) Focusing excessively on what a person wants to believe is true, or hopes is true, often obstructs clarification.

(e) Some people fear the clarification process because it might expose one's own hidden agenda, manipulative behavior, twisting of facts, and/or attempts to dominate or gain advantage.

The Goals of Clarification

The goal of clarifying is not to get everybody to agree on the same interpretations of a situation. The goals are to.......

- Expand and enrich understanding.
- Develop a comprehensive view of the overall situation.
- Gain a clearer understanding of the Self and Others.
- Clarify perceptions.....what they are, what they are based on, which are the same for the parties involved in a situation, and which are different.
- Discover what is factual and what is not. (More on Clarifying Facts will be presented later in this chapter.)
- Promote *mutual discovery*, rather than convincing others of our particular point of view. The clarification process is a shared endeavor, it is not one person dominating the process.
- Enrich communication by asking *effective questions*, not only by making statements.

Taking the last of the goals listed above, let's spend a little time on the art of asking effective questions. Effective dialogue and communication involves a good balance of questions and statements. Sadly, both formal and informal education pays little attention to what constitutes effective questions and how to phrase them.

Questions are a critical aspect of clarifying, so let's take a look at the art of asking quality questions.

Characteristics of Effective Questions

Effective questions.........

1. **Focus on the Broader Context first.** In any situation, it is important to begin with "Circle" questions, those focusing on the broader context. Doing so can help all parties (a) realize there is more to the situation than any single issue; (b) discover things that would otherwise be missed; and (c) identify any "Dots" that will eventually need to be addressed.

2. **Promote "Discovery".** Good clarifying questions promote mutual discovery, they are not "statement questions" which lead the other person toward a particular answer. Questions beginning with lead-ins such as, "Don't you think......", or "Shouldn't you do....." can easily be perceived as telling the other person what she or he should think or do. They are statements masquerading as questions.)

3. **Show genuine interest in the other person's needs, feelings, and perspectives.**

In all types of relationships and interactions, asking questions about the needs, feelings, and perceptions of the other people involved is crucial. It helps them realize we consider them to be just as important as we are in our dealings with each other. We need to make sure we phrase those questions in a way that does not sound like an interrogation or seem to be prying.

4. **Are Non-Threatening.** We can help clarify the realities of a situation without being threatening. For example, a threatening question is, "Don't you realize the damage you will cause if you do (X)?!" A non-threatening "discovery" question is, "What is your understanding of what could happen if (X) is done?" The response to that question often focuses on an outcome the person desires to happen. Then we can ask, "What if it that does not happen?" or "What other effects might that action produce?"

5. **Focus on Connectors early in the dialogue process.**
As you will remember, "connectors" are things that link people constructively to (a) each other, and/or (b) something they both need or care about.

6. Go from Broad to Specific. The process of dialogue usually gathers positive momentum and clarity if we begin with broader questions before moving to more specific content and questions. Through the broader questions we are able to discover and clarify the specifics in need of attention.

7. Avoid putting several issues in the same question. Asking a question that contains several issues usually confuses dialogue. It is much better to ask a question on one issue, and say this issue is linked to others we can discuss next.

8. Avoid Using "But" as a lead-in. Someone says something, and if we start our reply with "But...", it can leave the impression we are, in effect, saying, "What you just said is not acceptable or correct."

9. Use wise timing. When we ask certain questions is important. It has already been noted that asking broader questions and connector questions early helps the process of clarifying. The timing of when we ask *action* questions also needs emphasis.

10. Clarify Action Steps. *Action questions* focus on clarifying the action steps needed to deal with a situation. Action questions are usually more effective if asked after perceptions have been clarified and perhaps a Shared Need or goal has been discovered. The action will then be built on more solid ground, not on misperceptions, unclarified needs, and confusing goals.

Furthermore, action questions are most effective if they focus on *steps* to help build a process. For example, asking "What *beginning steps* do you think we can do together?" is more effective than asking a question like, "So what's the solution?"

11. Do not fear the expression of emotion. Questions that might lead to the expression of emotions will need to be asked. Emotions hold within them certain "messages" that need to be expressed. The LifeSkills help give us the capability of dealing with emotions effectively.

12. Accept the value of Silence. Moments of silence in dialogue can reflect that a person is thinking, or just pausing. So if a temporary silence follows one of our questions, we should not allow impatience or a fear of silence to grip us. That often leads to making an ill-advised statement or asking a frustrated question.

However, if the silence goes on too long, we need to consider we may have asked a question that was (a) too complex; (b) did not use wise timing; or (c) was threatening. After the silence, it is helpful to say, "While we were thinking, something came to my mind." Such a comment reinforces the belief that silence can be productive, not wasteful or uncomfortable. Then we can ask a good follow-up question.

Although there are many additional characteristics of effective questions, the ones mentioned above offer a dependable and practical foundation.

In the best of all worlds, everything involved in a situation should be clarified. Realizing that will not happen in most cases, let's look at a few of the most essential clarifications that need to be accomplished. They not only help us understand what is real and what is not, they also lead to the discovery of important factors that would otherwise remain hidden.

We will use a case study approach as we focus on the critical clarifications that need to be accomplished in any situation. I would also like for you to be thinking of examples from your own experience. Here's the format we will use.

First, the critical clarifications will be listed.
Second, the case we are using as an example will be described.
Third, we will apply LifeSkill #4 to the case.

Critical Clarifications

1. Clarify the Broader Context (the overall situation)
2. Clarify Perceptions
  - of the Self
  - of the Other
  - of the Relationship
  - of the specific Situation
3. Clarify Facts
4. Clarify What Needs To Be Done, Can Be Done, and How To Do It

(NOTE: This fourth item in the list is a LifeSkill on its own, LifeSkill #5, and is discussed at length in Chapter 5.)

The Case of the Co-Managers

Gail was in her fourth year as one of several project managers at Advanced Technologies (AdTech), a medium-size company. One of her fellow managers, a man named Curt, was also in his fourth year at the company. Gail usually received higher performance evaluations than Curt, and he frequently complained she was being favored because she was a woman. He was a rather impatient fellow and never liked taking time and energy to "clarify". Gail, on the other hand, understood the importance of clarifying and tried to use the skill.

    The company had a tradition of appointing co-managers to run projects. On March 1, AdTech's president appointed Gail and Curt to co-manage a new project, called Alpha. The project would need to be completed by March 31.

    At the same time, the president also made a surprise announcement. A new supervisory position in the company was being created. The position would not officially begin until June 1, but the decision on who would be promoted to the position would be announced on March 31, which happened to be the same date Alpha Project had to be completed. As the two most experienced managers in the company, Gail and Curt were the clear front runners for the new position, and they both strongly wanted to be the one selected.

The main steps involved in each critical clarification will now be described, then how they were or were not applied in the Case of the Co-Managers will be explored as we go through the case as it unfolds.

1. Clarify the Broader Context (the overall situation)

The Steps: LifeSkill #1, covered in our first chapter, uses a lot of clarification and discovery. Indeed, it is the clarification that needs to be done at the very beginning of any situation. Here is a brief review.

- Clarify there *is* a broader context containing <u>many</u> components. (People often see only what they choose to see, not the holistic "bigger picture", the "Circle".)
- Clarify what those components are. (Connectors, Needs, Resources, etc....see the graphic on the last page of Chapter 1 for review.)
- Clarify anything the various parties may be fixating on and turning into Dots.
- Clarify how the various components might affect each other.

Done individually first, then together with the other people or groups involved in a situation, clarifying the broader context provides a comprehensive foundation on which to move forward.

Applying the LifeSkill to the Case

    Gail and Curt met the day after being appointed co-managers of the Alpha Project and hearing about the creation of the new supervisory position. Gail suggested they start by clarifying the Broader Context, and even drew the Circle & Dot graphic on newsprint. Carl reluctantly agreed to go along with Gail's approach, provided it didn't take very long. Here's what they clarified, with Gail doing most of the work.

They filled in the Circle with the major components of the Broader Context, the overall situation.

(1) <u>Alpha Project</u>. They listed the things they would need to clarify about the project, including (a) the needs the project would serve; (b) the short-term and long-term goals; (c) the resources required and how to get them; (d) how to invite and utilize the input from the people who would be most affected by the project; (e) a reminder to themselves to make sure and do some initial "What If" planning in order to be prepared for various outcome levels....AND (f) the need to clarify their perceptions of the best way to divide up responsibilities as co-managers.

(2) <u>The New Supervisor Position</u>. Gail pointed out that the president's surprising announcement added a component to the overall situation. She asked Curt what effects competing for the position might have on their serving as effective co-managers in Alpha Project. Curt didn't answer, but Gail sensed wheels were turning in his mind. He had always demonstrated an obsession with "winning" at all costs, and she was concerned trouble might lie ahead. She didn't express her concern to him, deciding instead to state her priority. She told him she would focus on making Alpha successful and would not drain away energy from that responsibility by actively competing for the promotion.

(3) <u>Other Components</u>
- Perceptions (discussed in the next section)
- Facts (also discussed later)

NOTE: The president did not do a good job with one of the critical aspects of Clarifying the Broader Context; namely, how various components in the Circle might affect each other. For example, he did not clarify how Gail and Curt's co-manager performance might be affected by the fact they were now competitors for the new supervisory position. The president knew Gail and Curt were the front runners, and he knew Curt's history as an employee who did whatever was necessary to gain advantage over co-workers. But the president ignored those parts of the overall situation and went ahead and announced the position at the same time Alpha Project was beginning. The new position would not begin for three months, so he could have waited to make the announcement until the project was completed. If he had clarified how competing for the position might negatively affect Alpha Project, he would have waited.

2. Clarify Perceptions

Perceptions are the lenses through which people interpret the life around them. Perceptions affect our interpretations of reality, how we see ourselves and others, the opinions we form, and the actions we choose. With such a profound influence on every aspect of life, it is no wonder that Clarifying Perceptions is a major requirement if we want to be effective.

We all know that people can encounter the same situation and perceive it quite differently. Our experiences also tell us that all parties in an interaction do not need to have the same perceptions for the interaction to be effective. It is crucial, however, that perceptions are indeed *clarified*. If decisions and actions are based on perceptions that are unclear, or based only on assumptions and rumors, or are incorrect, it becomes more difficult to build mutually effective relationships and interactions, deal with problems, resolve conflicts, and accomplish any task successfully.

Every situation has its own set of perceptions that need to be clarified. However, there are several general categories of perceptions that apply to all situations. Let's look at each of those categories and some key questions that will serve us well. Some of the questions apply to more than one category and will be repeated.

Clarify Perceptions of the SELF

- "What do I *need*, not just what do I want? Might some of those needs be shared by _____ ?"(the other person or persons involved in the situation with me)
- "Is my behavior consistent with my values?"
- "On what am I basing my perceptions and interpretations?"
- "Am I giving conflicting signals to the people I am interacting with? Am I being clear enough?"
- "Am I fixating on any Dots to the detriment of the overall relationship (or interaction, or planning process, or task, etc.)?"
- "What parts of my total Identity 'connect' with parts of the other person's or group's total Identity, even though certain aspects of Identity are very different or even in conflict?"
- "How have I contributed to the problem?" Don't just look at how the other party has contributed to the problem.
- "I need to clarify how I can best remain in charge of myself and not allow the behavior of others to lead me to choose behavior I

know is not effective."
- "I need to be aware of my 'buttons' (those aspects of myself that, when pushed, tend to make me lose all reason), and to figure out ways to stop the escalation of damaging emotions within myself when my buttons are pushed."
- "Am I prepared to deal with <u>anger</u> directed at me?"

If another party directs anger at me, I need to clarify a few things within myself. One, anger is a form of energy, and that energy can be channeled in constructive ways. Two, there are usually important messages contained in the anger, often an expression of needs the other party is feeling. So I need to concentrate on and clarify those messages rather than being overcome by the yelling, angry facial expressions, etc. I need to look for something in one of those messages I can use to formulate a good question, a question that gets us working together constructively.

- "I need to remind myself that I will be more secure if I help my relationship and interaction partners also feel secure in their dealings with me."
- "When I am involved in conflicts, I need to clarify for myself if the conflict is actually an *Internal Conflict* within me, not a conflict with the other party."

Clarifying perceptions of the Self can help a person feel more secure, and can make relationships and interactions more effective. The same is true for clarifying perceptions of the other person or people involved with us.

Applying the LifeSkill to the Case

Gail immediately did some personal clarifying. She realized it would be tempting to divert her attention away from co-managing the project so she could spend time and energy trying to come up with a strategy for securing the new supervisor position. But she wisely clarified what giving in to that temptation would cause. One, it would violate one of her key values (doing each assignment with total commitment). Two, it would result in Alpha project being managed poorly, which would weaken the benefits for the people involved in the project. And three, as co-manager, the failure of the project would reflect poorly on her, thereby hurting her chances to be chosen for the supervisor position.

Carl did not do any significant clarifying of the "whole" Self. He fixated solely on his determination to "win" the promotion, and everything else became a tool toward that end. He did not clarify how fixating on that "Dot" and pursuing it ruthlessly might negatively affect other parts of his life. His performance as co-manager of Alpha, his relationship with Gail and other colleagues, how his wife and children might view him if they knew what he was doing....he ignored those important aspects of his life.

Instead, Curt began doing whatever he thought was necessary to get the promotion. He devoted his energy toward manipulating the co-manager responsibilities during the first two weeks of the project so he would look good and Gail would look bad. He purposely failed to complete a few of his co-manager tasks, then found opportunities to go to the president's office and drop little comments that hinted Gail was to blame.

Clarify Perceptions of the OTHER

- Focus on the other person/group's <u>total</u> Identity, not just one identity component.
- Ask, "What parts of my total Identity 'connect' with parts of the other person's or group's Identity, even though certain aspect of Identity are very different or even in conflict?"
- Focus on the "total" person, not only their most negative behavior.

As mentioned earlier, people and groups are more than just the negative behavior they are showing in a particular situation. Yet, it is quite easy and tempting to allow ourselves to become so bothered or threatened by that negative behavior that we "define" the other party by that negative behavior. Suddenly, the other party's positive potential is ignored. We need to clarify our perceptions of others rather than assuming or stereotyping them.

- In the midst of a situation in which the negative behavior of others is constantly on our minds, think of some positive act that person or group has done.
- Differentiate between the <u>personhood</u> of other people and their <u>behavior</u>. Focus on the <u>behavior</u> we are troubled by rather than on seeing and treating the personhood of the other party as our 'target' of criticism.
- Reach for the positive potential in others, and work with them to find specific action steps where that positive potential can be used.

Applying the LifeSkill to the Case

Curt did not clarify his perceptions of the Other. In this case,

Gail, the president, and the people involved in Alpha Project were the "others". He assumed Gail was as ruthlessly ambitious as he was and was secretly undermining him as he was undermining her. That led to his being even more ruthless as he tried to "do it to her before she can do it to me".

He also failed to clarify his perceptions of the president. Curt assumed his own values were shared by the president, specifically the value of ambitiously going after a goal at all costs. That assumption led Curt to convince himself the president would reward that kind of ambition by promoting Curt to the new supervisory position.

Gail also did an inadequate job of clarifying the "other". She did not want to believe Curt, as a person who had risen to the ranks of a project manager in the company, would stoop to unethical behavior at the expense of Alpha Project. She had never liked him as a person, but she wanted to respect him as a manager. So she never confronted him about what he was doing, why he felt such tactics were necessary, and how his actions might negatively affect him.

The next category is clarifying perceptions of the relationship. Since a clarified Self and clarified Other interact within a relationship, many of the suggestions already offered apply to this category as well. Here are a few additional items.

Clarify Perceptions of the RELATIONSHIP
- Clarify what the overall relationship or interaction *needs*, rather than only focusing on what I *want* in a particular situation.
- Clarify how a particular situation can be dealt with in a way that not only deals effectively with the present but also improves the relationship for the future.
- Clarify the relative importance a particular conflict has within the overall relationship or interaction. In other words, how "big" or "small" is a particular "Dot" in the "Circle" in terms of the effect that Dot has on the other important aspects of the relationship?
- Clarify the interrelationship between the short-term and the long-term. Do the short-term goals and actions lead to effective long-term goals and actions? *Satisfying certain self-serving desires or demands in the short-term may have damaging effects on the long-term health of a relationship or interaction.*
- Clarify how we need each other.
- In situations where there are significant conflicts with another

person or group, clarify those aspects of the relationship or interaction that are still *positive.*
- Asking the opinion of the other party <u>before</u> expressing one's own opinion can be a step in promoting a partnership atmosphere in a relationship or interaction.

Applying the LifeSkill to the Case

It is obvious both Gail and Curt gave inadequate attention to clarifying their perceptions of their relationship. How important their relationship was to the project, to the eventual decision about who would be promoted, how they might improve their relationship.....none of these was clarified or even considered. Curt saw the relationship only as a tool to use in winning the promotion, so he had little interest in improving the relationship.

Gail knew her relationship with Curt needed to be improved. Yet, she was so annoyed by his behavior she did not take the time and effort to explore with him the specific steps necessary to make improvements in their relationship.

Clarifying Perceptions of the SITUATION (additional comments)

Parties often perceive situations differently. As stated earlier, it is not necessary that all parties have the same perceptions. It is crucial, however, that they clarify what the perceptions are, what they are based on, which are the same or similar, and which are different. Here are some important questions to ask in Clarifying Perceptions of any situation. Again, some of these have already been mentioned.
- What's in the Broader Context, the Circle? Are other important components of the overall situation being ignored because I am focusing too much on only one part (a Dot), and is fixating on the Dot obstructing a clarification of the other components?
- *When we identify and clarify the components of a situation, it is important to choose which component we will deal with <u>first</u>. The initial component should usually be one that provides the best chance for cooperation, and can yield a feasible first step, however small that step may be.*
- One aspect of clarifying perceptions is making sure all the people involved in a particular interaction discuss their perceptions of what the ultimate goals are. If people are using the interaction for unclear or even conflicting purposes, it will not be effective for anybody.
- "What is the <u>process</u> we are going to use (rather than focusing on preconceived outcomes), and what are the first steps to get the

process started?"

3. Clarify FACTS

Dictionaries do a good job in providing basic definitions for most of the words and concepts that fill our lives. However, dictionaries are not so helpful in defining certain other words and concepts, and I suggest "fact" is one of them. Here's how one respected dictionary defines the word.

Fact: (1) something known to have occurred or to be true; (2) the quality of being actual; (3) the statement of something done or known to be true. As I ponder the definition, I find three words in need of more clarity: "known", "true", and "actual". What happens if there is no agreement on what is "known" or on what is "true"? What does "actual" mean, and how do we tell if something is actual? If it's not actual, it's.... what? "Non-actual", just a figment of creative imagination?

This meandering discussion is intended to point out the complexity we face in the seemingly simple step of Clarifying Facts. Some folks may contend it really IS simple, that something is either a fact or it's not because facts are absolute. They think they are clear on what the absolute facts are, and anyone who disagrees is wrong.

Progress and cooperation is still possible even in situations where people disagree on what is known, what is true, what is actual. Several general questions get us started in the clarification of facts. (NOTE: These questions aid mutual discovery, which, as already mentioned, is a critical aspect of clarifying.)

- The most basic question: *"On what am I (or you or we) basing that opinion (or interpretation or belief)?"* Even though it's a simple, vital, and the most fundamental clarifying question, it often goes unasked. We are then left with a rather lazy and tempting alternative: namely, substituting assumptions, rumors, illusions, and selective memory for facts.
- Dealing with "Facts" based on "actual events." A person in a group says, "It's a fact because it's based on an actual event people saw happen." Questions to clarify things further could be, *"Who are the people who saw it happen? Did you see it? Is there a record of it anywhere?"* These questions tend to be more effective than saying, "Prove it!"
- "Facts" based on beliefs or faith. This is a tough one. On the one hand, we all have a right to our beliefs, and we also have a right to take things on faith even though there is no "factual" evidence. On the other hand, trouble arises when people act as though whatever they take on faith is the same as a fact, and then expect everybody else to do the

same.

This dilemma will no doubt be with us always. I have found a good way to deal with such situations is through the following statement:

"You have told me you are basing some of your perceptions on what you believe to be true and on faith. I respect your right to do that, and I hope you can respect my need for us to be clear on what we <u>both</u> can accept is based on <u>fact</u>. I suggest we focus on those first, then see how the things you take on faith can enrich our efforts."

(NOTE: The question, "What are some things we both need or agree on that can help us move forward?" applies to all situations in which there is a disagreement on what is fact and what is not.)

Applying the LifeSkill to the Case

A few basic facts in the AdTech situation were clear to everyone involved.

FACT: Alpha Project needed to be completed by March 31.

FACT: The new supervisor would be announced on March 31, but the position would not officially begin until June 1.

Most of the other ingredients in the situation were left open to assumption, presumption, and interpretation. To give but two examples, the criteria used in selecting the new supervisor were not clearly stated; and the president did not clarify whether or not Curt's accusations against Gail had any basis in fact.

The Outcome of the Case

In spite of Curt's behavior, Gail was able to save Alpha project through long hours of diligent effort. The project ended on March 31 as scheduled, and that afternoon the president announced Gail would be the one promoted to the position of supervisor.

Curt was shocked. He thought he had set Gail up for failure, planted doubts about her in the president's mind, and cleverly manipulated the situation. His lack of clarifying hurt whatever chance he had to be promoted.

I would like to end our chapter on LifeSkill #4, *Clarify*, with a brief discussion of another actual case. It involves two teachers.

Case #2: The Teachers

The setting is a school, and the conversation we will eavesdrop on is between two teachers, Maud and Denise, who are as different as two people can be.

Maud is near retirement, very authoritarian with students, and intolerant of most everything other than her own very rigid life style. Denise is only two years out of graduate school, conducts a participatory classroom, and is what Maud calls "a reckless holdover Hippie".

Last week, Robin, one of Maud's students, needed personal advice. She chose to go to Denise, not Maud. Maud was irate. She confronted Denise in the hall outside their classrooms, and many students heard the loud outburst.

During the next week, rumors spread that the two teachers, whose classrooms were next to each other, almost got in a fight. Denise finally asked Maud to discuss their situation privately after school in one of the empty classrooms. Here is a small part of their interaction.

(M=Maud, D=Denise)

M: You're a disgrace to the teaching profession! Your clothes are too suggestive, your classroom is too loud...and how dare you fill the mind of one of MY students with your liberal nonsense!

D: Maud, I'd like to understand why you and I seem to have a rocky professional relationship, and what we can do to improve it. I believe students deserve to have their teachers be good examples in how relationships are conducted.

M: Then change your ways!

D: Which "ways"? You've mentioned the way I dress, the way I teach, my being available to students like Robin when they come to talk to me....let's clarify what's going on here.

M: I'm sure Robin talked to you about me, and you tried to make her dislike me.

D: That's not what happened, but she wants to keep our conversation confidential, and I'm respecting her wishes. You can ask her what we talked about if you want, and let her decide if she wants to tell you. But I'd like go back to my question. What do you think is making our relationship so difficult? If we can clarify that, maybe we can improve things."

M: It's...it's a lot of things.

D: Let's start with one we can deal with....like Robin's coming to talk to me. Why does that upset you?

M: She's MY student! And....and I worry about the advice you might give her.

D: Would you feel comfortable asking her why she came to me?

M: (Silence)
D: If a student from someone else's class came to you for advice, would you turn her away?
M: They wouldn't come to me. Compared to you, they think I'm cold and heartless. You make it difficult for me.
D: I'm not trying to make it difficult for you, Maud. You can give good advice, too. I think maybe the students see you not socializing with other teachers and start perceiving you as someone they can't talk to. I don't perceive you that way.
M: You don't?
D: No, I don't. I think we need to give ourselves a chance to get to know the real you and the real me. Any suggestions on how we might do that?
M: Well...I guess we could visit each other's classrooms to see how each of us teaches.
D: I like that idea. And maybe we could collaborate on some kind of school activity?

Denise helped create an atmosphere in which a lot of effective clarifying could be done.
- The negative effect the current Denise-Maud relationship was having on two things both cared about---the students and the school---was an important clarification.
- Why Maud disliked her and what that dislike was based on.
- Maud's incorrect perceptions about the conversation Denise had with Robin.
- Possible reasons why students did not feel comfortable going to Maud for advice.
- Possibilities to work together to improve their professional relationship.

Clarifying is a LifeSkill we need to use constantly throughout any relationship, any interaction.

Chapter 5

LifeSkill #5: Focus on What <u>Needs</u> To Be Done, <u>Can</u> Be Done, and <u>How</u> to Do It (the NCH LifeSkill)

*The endless pursuit
of Desire's tempting charms
so often creates
murky clouds
obscuring the needs
we could have seen,
and then we expend
our precious time
trying to force
a rock to sprout leaves
as we struggle to climb
the rugged terrain
without building paths
of steppingstones.*

"Focus on What **N**eeds To Be Done, **C**an Be Done, and **H**ow To Do It" is a very functional LifeSkill. It also has a long name (15 letters). So to save me from having to repeat the full title numerous times, and to save you from having to read it over and over again, I will do us both a favor and sometimes use the abbreviation, "NCH". Doing so might also provide a handy way to remember the LifeSkill, akin to how the Circle & Dot image helps us remember LifeSkill #1.

With that introduction out of the way, let's begin our exploration of LifeSkill #5. If we keep the importance of NCH front and center in our minds, we will be much more effective and efficient. If, on the other hand, we fail to focus on what needs to be done, can be done, and how to do it, negative results usually occur.

- Important needs go unrecognized, and/or the difference between needs and desires becomes cloudy.
- Time and energy is spent on pursuits we do not have the power and resources to accomplish.
- We stumble along aimlessly without the practical, proven skills essential to effectiveness.

Outlined below are the components of the NCH LifeSkill.
1. **Focus on NEEDS and What Needs To Be Done**
   a. **Differentiate between Needs and Desires**
   b. **Individual Needs**
   c. **Shared Needs**
   d. **Focusing on Needs and Proposals, rather than Demands**
2. **Focus on What CAN Be Done**
3. **Focus on HOW To Do It (also covered in LifeSkill #6)**
   a. **The LifeSkills**
   b. **"Power-WITH"** (TM)

1. Focus on What NEEDS To Be Done
An Overview of "Needs"

The concept of "needs" has been explored in numerous volumes through the years, and I will not attempt to summarize or examine those valuable contributions. Rather, I will offer a functional definition of "needs" as an overview.

I suggest human needs can be defined as follows:

NEEDS are resources essential for (1) survival; (2) positive development beyond mere survival ("survival-plus needs"); and (3) building and sustaining mutually beneficial relationships.

The first category of needs in the definition is obvious. Survival depends on getting certain basic needs met. Tragically, many members of human society are in such disadvantaged conditions that meeting even the most basic survival needs is a constant struggle.

For those of us who are able to count on our basic survival needs being met, we spend a lot of time and energy securing the second category, "survival-plus needs". They are the needs required to go beyond mere survival and develop more and more of our potential.

The third category, "building and sustaining mutually beneficial relationships", is not generally considered to be a "need". However, I suggest it is indeed a need for our highly social species. We spend a majority of life in relationships and interactions. The quality of our lives is greatly enhanced when those relationships and interactions provide <u>mutual</u> benefits. In other words, if we are to have a fulfilled, quality life, we <u>need</u> to be able to work well with others.

Differentiate between Needs and Desires

In focusing on What Needs to be Done, one of the first steps is to differentiate between needs and desires. One respected dictionary defines the two concepts as follows.

"Desire": (1) the feeling that a person would derive pleasure or satisfaction by obtaining or possessing something; and (2) an expressed wish.

"Need": a requirement; something that is necessary.

Even without the help of a dictionary, we all know intellectually that needs and desires are not synonymous. Yet people often confuse the two. The most problematic confusion comes when we elevate the pursuit of desires to a level of importance that should be reserved for the meeting of needs.

When that happens, it becomes easier to justify trying to satisfy a desire at all costs because we convince ourselves it is a "need". In doing so, we create confusion in ourselves and in our interactions with others. We also make it more difficult to focus on actual needs.

We all have desires, of course, and satisfying them can give us pleasure. The challenge is to understand that desires and needs are not synonymous, to distinguish between needs and desires, and to focus on needs as being most important.

Let's take a few examples, some rather obvious, some not so obvious. As we do, let's keep in mind a critical fact: *pursuing and satisfying certain desires can obstruct the meeting of certain needs.*

• Carl <u>needs</u> to travel from point A to point B, but <u>desires</u> to make the trip in a Porsche. Walking, using a bicycle, taking a taxi or bus, or driving a less fancy car would all meet the <u>need</u>.

• Stan <u>needs</u> to maintain a happy relationship with his spouse or partner or children, but <u>desires</u> to have his own way in most every aspect of the relationship. His desire for dominance and his domineering behavior obstruct the meeting of his need for a good relationship.

• For reasons of human health, sustainable resource availability, and long-term economic profit, a company <u>needs</u> to be environmentally responsible. The company <u>desires</u> immediate, temporary, short-term profits, so spends next to nothing on environmental protection policies. The ultimate results? Cleanup costs wipe out the short-term profits, and consumers might even boycott the company.

• A multi-racial community <u>needs</u> to provide educational opportunities for all its youth regardless of race. However, the community leaders (who are members of the dominant race) <u>desire</u> to perpetuate their dominance. They allocate twice as many resources to the dominant race schools and after-school programs as are allocated to minority race schools. Some of the results are inadequate education for the disadvantaged youth, their inability to get jobs, racial tension, and even youth gang violence.

All of us can come up with numerous and no doubt better examples of the difference between needs and desires. The point, however, should be clear. Needs and desires are not the same, and allowing desires to become more important than needs leads to problems.

I have found there are two rather basic questions we can ask to help clarify the difference between needs and desires.

1. Whenever there is something we are perceiving as a need, we can ask, *If I don't get what I think I am "needing", how will I be damaged?* If we have a hard time coming up with ways we will be damaged, then what we are perceiving as a "need" is probably a desire.

2. Many people fall into the habit of using the words "need" and "want" interchangeably. In situations where we are trying to identify and understand needs, we can make sure and ask, "What do I need?" rather than "What do I want?", and "What do you need?", rather than "What do you want?"

There are two basic categories of needs present in every relationship and interaction: Individual Needs and Shared Needs.

INDIVIDUAL Needs

It might seem logical to assume individuals or groups clearly understand their own needs in any particular situation. I think we all know such an assumption is not always correct. Part of the reason is the lack of differentiation between needs and desires discussed above, and part of the reason is a failure to "Clarify Perceptions of the Self" discussed in Chapter 4.

Individual needs vary, of course, depending on the situation and the people involved. However, there are certain Individual Needs we can identify as being critical to every person and every effective relationship and interaction. In other words, all parties involved have these individual needs. If these basic individual needs are met, a solid foundation will be established for moving forward constructively.

Individual Needs Critical for Every Person and Every Effective Relationship/ Interaction

- Being <u>perceived for who we are in our totality</u>, not as an image based on only one part of our identity, or only one behavior we have committed, or stereotypes.
- Being able to <u>express ourselves</u> if we so choose, and being <u>listened to</u> with respect even if what we are expressing disagrees with the listener's point of view.
- Clarity on what our own needs are, and clarity on the needs of our interaction partners.
- Finding <u>action steps</u> to deal with a situation, not merely intellectualizing.
- Working in <u>partnership</u> with interaction partners on a situation that affects all of us.
- Discovering "Shared Needs" (see below).

The second category of needs is what I call "Shared Needs".

SHARED Needs

Shared Needs are needs all parties have in common.
Shared Needs are "connectors" in the midst of divisions.
Shared Needs help people and groups realize they need each

other if shared goals are to be accomplished and interactions are to prove effective.

Shared Needs can serve as "building blocks" for cooperation in planning, problem-solving, conflict resolution, and many other challenges.

In conflicts, Shared Needs can be a powerful foundation on which to build a transformation of the conflict from a negative competition for "victory" to an opportunity to clarify and improve a situation for mutual benefit.

Focusing on Needs and Proposals, rather than Demands

An entire book could be devoted to this complex topic and still only scratch the surface. I will limit myself to a brief discussion of what I believe are the most relevant considerations.

First, people often think their demands are expressing needs, and in some cases that may indeed be true. However, in many situations demands express desires rather than needs. The person or group making the demands tries to create the impression that critical needs are involved and, therefore, the demands should be met. This frequently used strategy makes the identification of actual needs more difficult.

Second, experience tells us that making demands often produces ineffective interaction, for the following reasons.

(1) Using demands almost always promotes defensiveness. Each party devotes energy toward defending its own demands, rather than finding Shared Needs on which mutual benefit cooperation can be developed.

(2) Demands are sometimes used as a tactic to make the other party appear to be the one obstructing progress. It works this way. The one making the demands does not want progress, so makes demands that are so extreme and one-sided there is no way the other party can possibly agree to those demands. Then the demanding party says, "See? It's your fault. You refuse to cooperate."

(3) Even in situations where we believe there is justification in issuing demands, *suggesting constructive "proposals" is more effective and ultimately more powerful than making demands*. Proposals open up possibilities for cooperative action, whereas demands do just the opposite.

We now turn to the second component of LifeSkill #5.

2. Focus on What <u>Can</u> Be Done

An initial question arises. How do we know what we <u>can</u> do (what is within our capability) and what we cannot do?

I firmly believe humanity has developed only a small percentage of our potential, and numerous studies agree. Providing statistical proof for such an assertion might be difficult, but several things seem clear. One, humans have not been around very long in the total flow of existence on Earth. Two, the cerebral cortex in humans gives us wondrous possibilities for advancement. Three, our exponential leaps in discovering and utilizing our potential indicate there is a lot of untapped potential still awaiting development.

One might ask, "So what?" We are still left with the question, "How do we know what we can do and cannot do?" Several guidelines seem crucial as we try to deal with this question.

1. <u>Focus on exploring possibilities before focusing on limitations</u>. If we begin with a focus on why something can <u>not</u> be done, we usually ignore creative possibilities for how it <u>might</u> be done. We also dampen our enthusiasm and fail to initiate momentum.

2. If there is something we need to do, yet feel we do not have the capability to do it, <u>explore ways to expand our capabilities so we can do it</u>. Developing additional skills within ourselves, or adding people with key skills to our group or task, or finding a way to get other needed resources....all can be explored. We just might turn a "can't do" into a "can do".

3. <u>After following the first two guidelines, we then need to come to grips with what we actually can do, not just on what we would like to do</u>. After expanding our horizons through the creative exploration of possibilities, after gathering additional capabilities, we need to look realistically at what is within our power to accomplish. People often expend a lot of time and energy focusing on things that are not within <u>their</u> power to accomplish. We need to do as well as possible those things we can do, and try to encourage others who may have the power to go ahead and do those things we ourselves cannot do.

4. <u>Do not allow the Past to hold the Present and Future hostage</u>. If in the Past a particular task was unsuccessful, or cooperation didn't occur, we are not doomed to the same result in the Present and Future. With more insight, better skills, and a good process, we might produce more effective, quality outcomes.

5. <u>Make effective suggestions</u> which (a) involve mutual benefits; (b) can be done by the other people or groups involved with us in a situation; and (c) *do not depend on some outside person or structure we cannot* *realistically influence.* If these ingredients are built into suggestions, the suggestions have a better chance of being things we <u>can</u> do.

  6. <u>Consider if a particular task can be done in the time frame available.</u> If not, that task may have to be done later, and/or we may need to alter the time frame if possible. Considering the time frame influences our decisions about which steps are most feasible now, and which will come later.

  7. <u>Focus on the specific "how-to" necessary to do what needs to be done and can be done</u>......which leads us to the next component of the NCH LifeSkill.

3. Focus on <u>How</u> To Do It

Building solid relationships, developing happy families, improving organizations, being successful in our jobs, building lives of quality..... I am sure we all share these and other important goals. Accomplishing these goals requires not only our commitment and perseverance, it also requires the wisdom and skills to determine <u>how</u> to accomplish these and other goals. Implementing the "how-to" then requires action, and the engine of action is.....Power.

Exploring "POWER"

At its generic root, "power" is defined as "the capacity to perform effectively". Yet, our perceptions and uses of power have added many complex layers to that basic definition. Understanding what power means in our lives, and choosing how we use it, greatly influences every human endeavor.

There are two basic categories of Power: Personal Power and what I will term Interaction Power, the power we use in our relationships and interactions. The two categories affect each other, of course, but also have characteristics of their own.

PERSONAL Power

"When do you feel powerful?" is a question I ask in my training workshops throughout the world. Before I list the most frequent responses, I would like for you to ask yourself that question and give it some thought.

Now that you have had time to consider your own responses,

here are the ones I most frequently get in my workshops, regardless of who the participants are and the culture from which they come.
"I feel powerful when I.....
....feel confident."
....have the knowledge and skills I need in a particular situation."
....am in control of a situation and can get what I want."
....set goals and accomplish them."
....feel secure."
....win. In a competition, a conflict, a debate...anything."
....can make other people do what I want them to do."
....can protect myself and those people I care about."
....can deal with conflicts."

These responses clearly reveal there are perceptions of "power" shared by people throughout the world. The responses also show that some aspects of one's own Personal Power are linked to interactions with other people (Interaction Power), but for now let's look at some suggestions for developing the personal power essential to quality living.

Developing Personal Power

Using all of the LifeSkills we have been discussing helps make us more constructively powerful. Developing personal power also involves other steps.

- Clarify the values and priorities we want to guide our lives and try to apply them in daily living.
- Expand and diversify knowledge, including the learning of specific skills.
- Understand the broader context of situations, rather than fixating on "Dots".
- Take responsibility for our own actions.
- Develop and use constructive Interaction Power.

INTERACTION Power

I suggest there are two basic kinds of Interaction Power: "Power-Over", and what I term "Power-WITH".

"Power-Over"

As used in this book, *the term "Power-Over" refers to the kind of power that seeks to dominate, or gain control over others, rather than trying to build mutual benefit cooperation.*

Perceiving "power" as Power-Over, and using it in a relationship or interaction, usually has three major results.

One, an "I versus you" atmosphere is created. The possibility of "we working together" is not considered.

Two, doing whatever is perceived as necessary to "win" the battle and get more power-over the other person or group becomes the interaction pattern.

Three, the competition to gain controlling advantage usually involves trying to weaken the other party. In other words, it "subtracts" from the total power that potentially exists in a relationship or interaction.

"Power-WITH"

In the early years of my work, I coined the term "Power-WITH" to try to provide a simple, clear, action-oriented picture of one of the ways we can perceive and use "power". Another way this kind of power can be described is "shared positive power".

Power-WITH is the energy that creates partnership and mutual benefit cooperation. It makes all parties stronger. Developing and using Power-WITH is an essential LifeSkill in making our relationships and interactions effective.

Power-WITH is stronger than any other kind of power. It is "power addition" because your positive power is added to my positive power. The total power we have together is increased.

Practical Steps in Developing "Power-WITH"

- Be conscious of the differences between Power-WITH and Power-Over, and realize it is our choice as to which kind of power we will try to use.
- Communicate to the other party that "we need each other" to make this interaction or situation effective and to produce needed and sustainable outcomes.
- Make as many "We" statements as possible.
- Focus on a particular Shared Need or goal and say, "We have agreed on _____ (the shared need or goal), but we have not been able to accomplish it by working against each other. Let's focus on working with each other and see if we can accomplish it."
- Focus on and develop <u>specific</u>, "Doable" action steps using Power-WITH. (See the LifeSkill, "Develop Doables" in Chapter 6)

- Even if the other party tries to create a battle for Power-Over, stay committed to inviting and implementing Power-WITH.
- Believe in, and work for, <u>mutual</u> benefits.
- *Realize that just because somebody else benefits, that does not mean I "lose" anything.*
- Use all the LifeSkills presented in this book.

An Example of Developing Power-WITH

There are countless examples of the Power-WITH process, one of which occurred in the 1980's in a country that was characterized by extreme racial separation and discrimination. The country was ruled harshly by the minority race, which constituted only 15% of the national population. The communities were strictly divided by race, and the towns where the majority race lived were greatly disadvantaged because the resources of the country were monopolized by the minority race. Those communities had inferior schools and houses, no electricity, and no adequate access to water. There were no government-funded development projects. All of the deplorable conditions were the result of the national policy designed, implemented and tightly controlled by the minority race.

I was invited by the leaders of the oppressed race to work in some of their communities. In one extremely poor town, I was taking a long walk to do some thinking. Gradually, more and more people fell in step with me, and we started talking.

"See?" one man said as we looked at the awful conditions. "We have nothing, and the government wants to keep it that way. We have no resources to do anything."

"Let's talk more about that," I suggested. "Are there any things you might not think of as resources, but you might turn into something useful?"

"No", a few citizens answered.

I asked the same question again. "Well," a young woman answered tentatively, "maybe it's not really a resource, but.....Have you noticed all the pieces of cloth lying around?"

I had indeed noticed, and asked where they came from.

"We hand down our clothes to family members or other people who need them," another woman explained. "Then when the clothes are so worn out they can't be used any more, we just throw them on the ground. There aren't any trash services here, so we just throw the clothes away."

The ground was littered with discarded pieces of clothing, finally worn out by the youngest family member who was the last in line in the hand-me-down trail the clothes followed.

"How could you use those pieces of cloth?" I asked.

"They're useless," one person answered. "That's why we threw them away."

"You mean every part of each garment is useless?" I asked.

"Well...no. I guess little pieces of some of the clothes might still be good."

"How could they be used?" I asked.

The group thought for a few seconds, then one teenage woman said, "Maybe we could make some kind of shoulder bag or purse. You know...cut out the still usable parts of the garments, and sew those patches together to make bags or purses."

An important first step had been taken in developing the individual power of the villagers even though the government tried to keep them powerless. Given the lifelong feeling of having no power, a few people were understandably skeptical

"That would require a sewing machine," one man pointed out, focusing on obstacles rather than possibilities. "We don't have any machines. Even if we did, we don't have electricity."

"Who does have sewing machines," I asked, "the kind that don't require electricity?"

"*They* do," came the reply, meaning the dominant race.

"Do you have any contact with them?" I asked.

"Sure," one woman answered. "Many of us work as Domestics in their homes in the city."

I let the comment sink into the thinking process for a full fifteen seconds. Then I asked, "Do any of you have pretty good personal relationships with the people you work for? You know....as people, in spite of being from different races?"

"I do," the teenage woman said, showing some excitement. "The woman I work for has a teenage daughter about my age. She understands we aren't treated fairly. Maybe I could ask her if we could use one of her spare sewing machines, one she no longer uses. I've seen one or two in the garage."

"None of those people want anything to do with us," somebody scoffed. "It's foolish to get our hopes up by suggesting such impossible ideas."

"Well, I'm going to do it," the teenager said with determination.

"I think a lot of us should at least try."

And try they did. Within a month, ten peddle-powered sewing machines not requiring electricity were donated to the community by women of the dominating race. Within 6 months, more than 1,500 shoulder bags had been produced, and ten new communities were ready to join the project. Other members of the ruling race agreed to sell the bags in their city shops and give the full proceeds to the most depressed communities....proving once again there are always some people in an oppressor group who can be reached if Power-WITH is actively pursued.

Within two years the project had brought in enough income to build new schools in several of the communities, provide running water and electricity, and repair many houses. The people of the ruling race who were participants in the program began pressuring the government to repeal some of the more racist laws. A project that began in one community, primarily because it combined individual power and Power-WITH, became one of the early "steppingstones" in the process that eventually ended the system of racial discrimination in the society.

We have all experienced how Power-WITH can help improve our interactions. Yet, we often do not use it, turning instead to negative Power-Over. Why? Here are some possible reasons.

Reasons We Fail To Choose and Use Power-WITH
1. The Myth, "If you get anything, that means I'm losing something".

Many people are brought up believing that life is basically one competition after another, especially in conflict situations, and that "winning" is the primary goal. To "win", the other party's benefits must be kept to a minimum, or prevented completely. The structures and systems of highly competitive societies perpetuate and even reward such thinking. From among the many problems that result from this approach, two stand out.

One, people who conduct their interactions as power-over competitions for dominance limit the constructive potential of relationships and interactions. Even if they achieve dominance, they set in motion a pattern in which the full contribution of the other party is diminished. *Both parties are denied the benefits of that full contribution, thus both parties "lose" something.*

Second, "winning" in interactions usually results in the "losing" party either seeking revenge, or not supporting the outcome of the interaction with a sense of commitment.

The most effective relationships and interactions are those in which all the participants involved (a) have significant input, and (b) benefit in some way. If we build a Partnership Process, those mutual benefit outcomes are far more likely. Rather than trying to prevent the other participants from getting benefits because of the false belief "I will lose something", *we make our interactions most effective when we work just as hard to help others benefit as we do in gaining benefits for ourselves.*

2. The Myth, "Sharing power will somehow result in my looking weak because either I or others (or both) will think I'm not capable of doing it myself"; or "Using Power-WITH will diminish my receiving credit and being rewarded".

The reality is something quite different. In interactions, the people who are the most respected and have the most sustainable "strength" are those who use power cooperatively for the good of the interaction.

3. Some highly competitive societies do not emphasize cooperation, choosing instead to instill in citizens from an early age those attitudes and strategies that promote Power-Over.

Even though we may grow up in a society where learning how to use Power-Over is prevalent, we can choose to develop the attitudes and skills of Power-WITH in ourselves, our children, our families, and our educational systems.

As we draw near the end of Chapter 5, let's look at another actual case, this one combining the three components of the NCH LifeSkill, Focus on What Needs To Be Done, Can Be Done, and How To Do It. The names of the people, town, and organizations have been changed, but everything else happened as described below.

SOCK, BOP and the Centerville Commons

Welcome to Centerville. Nestled in a lovely valley where happy brooks babble and soft breezes blow, the town of 30,000 has long been considered a pleasant community. One of its most prized features is a large park in the center of town known as Centerville Commons. Citizens of all types have used the park for generations, enjoying picnics, jogging, playing sports, riding bicycles, watching children frolic, and just relaxing. The park has also had the long-standing tradition of hosting monthly concerts featuring local musicians. As one Centerville wag puts it, the local musicians "are more down-and-out than up-and-coming, but what the heck, they're our own".

Some of you may be thinking Paradise has finally been found. Others of you with more exotic tastes may be convinced a 21st Century Shangri-La has been discovered. Sadly, I must dispel both of those notions. For, you see, Centerville does have a few problems. "So what?" we might ask. "Hasn't every human settlement since the dawn of time had a few problems? Can't even perpetual Paradise get a bit boring sometimes?"

Boredom is not one of Centerville's problems, but rising unemployment is. Another is the demise of a few small businesses. Those two worries have been present for the past two years. Then a month ago, a third problem emerged. "Erupted" is probably a more correct description. Here's what happened.

Some local business owners got together and formed an organization they named the "Business Owners Progress Group". Since the acronym "BOPG" was not very catchy (and quite hard to pronounce with the "G" at the end), they shortened it to "BOP".

BOP proposed a plan to deal with the two economic problems. They proposed building a small shopping mall that would cover about half of the Centerville Commons park. Jobs would be created, and new businesses might be attracted to set up shop in the park. Furthermore, BOP argued, "location and convenience" are twin pillars of marketing, so maybe some of the new businesses would start stocking jogging apparel, biking equipment, and picnic supplies. Park users, on their way to, during and from participating in those activities, could conveniently stop and buy, buy, buy.

Given the fact Centerville Commons had been a near sacred feature of the town for almost 180 years, it was no wonder BOP's proposal prompted the formation of another citizens group. The group took the name "Save Our Commons". Desiring an appropriate acronym to counteract BOP, the new group came up with "SOCK". (The "K" was added in an attempt to give the acronym more clout.)

SOCK's agenda focused on preserving and protecting the beloved Commons. Generations of citizens had enjoyed the tranquility, open space, fresh air, and recreational delights of the park, and future generations deserved the same. To SOCK, allowing the park to be disgraced, scarred and polluted by putting a shopping mall on the hallowed grounds would be a sin, not to mention a dereliction of civic stewardship.

The SOCK and BOP debate rapidly gained momentum, turning

downright nasty. The normally happy-go-lucky citizens of Centerville took sides, some seeing SOCK as the protector of the Commons and champions of environmental values, others seeing BOP as the savior of the economy. The town's historic newspaper, The Centerville Voice, published Letters to the Editor that reminded town historians of the famous pistol duels fought on the Commons during the town's earliest years.

Afraid her wonderful town was tearing itself apart, Mayor Fran Whitmore sought help. I had met Fran when she attended a workshop I conducted on the LifeSkills at a national conference involving, among other participants, quite a few mayors from around the U.S. During the workshop, I gave a few examples taken from my work as what I call a Conflict Partnership Catalyst (CPC). Briefly summarized, that refers to the conflict resolution process I developed years ago and use as a comprehensive alternative to traditional mediation.

Fran called my office and asked if I would go to Centerville and serve as the CPC in the SOCK and BOP dilemma. She said she wanted me in Centerville in two days. My schedule was full with prior commitments for the next two weeks, so, reluctantly, I had to decline her kind invitation. I told her I believed she could deal with the situation effectively.

She asked if she could call back that night to discuss the matter thoroughly as part of her preparation. I readily agreed, she called later, and during the hour-long conversation, she described the Centerville situation thoroughly. We went over the material she had kept from the workshop, and we discussed in greater specificity how the LifeSkills could be applied.

When I returned from my trip, I called Fran to find out what had happened in Centerville. Before relating what Fran told me, *let me emphasize that although we are using this example to highlight LifeSkill #5 (the NCH LifeSkill), all of the LifeSkills come into play if we want to be effective.* With that in mind, we will summarize how the first four LifeSkills were used, then spend more time on the use of the NCH LifeSkill.

We are ready now to see what actually happened, as reported to me in detail by the mayor.
(From here on I'll refer to her as Fran, not "the mayor".) She arranged an all-day meeting in her office with the head of SOCK (Kris) and the main leader of BOP (Walt). Here is a summary of the meeting, presented under the LifeSkills headings.

1. The Broader Context (the Bigger Picture)

Fran utilized the Circle & Dot image to help the two leaders identify and consider the components of the Broader Context, not remain fixated on their respective Dots (building the shopping mall versus no shopping mall). As they "filled in the Circle", several key components of the bigger picture emerged, components both Walt and Kris agreed were critical.

- Both Kris and Walt cared deeply for the community they had lived in all their lives.
- The need to restore calm to the town, and to restore the cooperative interactions Centerville's citizens had always enjoyed.
- The importance of dealing effectively with the town's economic problems.
- The many benefits Centerville Commons provided the community.
- The fact Kris and Walt had been friends for years, and most of the SOCK and BOP members had also been friends for years and continued to be in spite of recent events.
- The shared commitment to be effective community leaders and set positive examples.
- The role of the media and how it was inflaming a "we versus them" mentality.

2. Focus on Connections

Fran asked questions that helped Kris and Walt see how all of the components of the Broader Context were connected, especially how the entire community was being negatively affected by the way SOCK and BOP were handling the situation. In other words, fixating on their respective Dots was damaging all the other components of the Broader Context.

3. Develop Secure I, Secure Other, Secure We

Fran was already planting seeds of LifeSkill #3 from the very beginning of the meeting. Kris and Walt had always been secure in their personal friendship, but as the leaders of SOCK and BOP they had become less secure with each other. Their proven friendship, their agreement on the components of the Broader Context, and the many connectors.....all helped Kris and Walt feel a bit more secure. They began to realize they could carry that feeling of being secure in their interactions as leaders of the two organizations.

4. Clarify

A lot needed to be clarified (LifeSkill #4: Clarify), and Fran asked questions to help in the clarification process. Here is a sample sequence of questions asked by Fran (F), followed by the responses from either BOP's leader, Walt (W) or SOCK's leader, Kris (K).

> F: What were BOP's reasons for choosing the park as the location for the shopping mall?
> W: It's a big area with a lot of potential shoppers every day.
> F: What other areas has BOP considered?
> W: Well....none. We think the park's the best location.
> F: Kris? What does SOCK think about the general idea of a small shopping mall?
> K: It might be good for the economy, but insisting it be put in the park ruins the idea.
> W: But there aren't any other places.
> F: Do we know that for sure? You said no other locations have even been considered.

Because BOP has been fixating on building the mall in the park, and SOCK has been fixating on saying "No!" to that plan, both groups have failed to consider the obvious and basic questions Fran asked. Through raising these questions, Fran gave Walt and Kris an opportunity to clarify a critical possibility: there may be a way to build a small shopping mall AND preserve the park. In other words, it may not be a rigid "either my way or your way" situation.

A series of effective clarifying questions usually leads to the use of LifeSkill #5: What Needs To Be Done, Can Be Done, and How To Do It.

5. What Needs To Be Done, Can Be Done, and How To Do It

As mentioned earlier, the main purpose behind discussing the Centerville case is to highlight LifeSkill #5, the NCH LifeSkill. Look how Fran applied that LifeSkill.

What Needs To Be Done

> F: Based on what we've done thus far, what are some of the things you as community leaders and heads of your organizations need to do?
> K: We need to find a way to work together for the good of our community. I guess I hadn't realized how our example has fed such

severe divisions among the citizens. We also need to preserve the park as a place of recreation....and we need to get creative and deal better with our economic problems.

W: I agree. Those are the things we need to do. But can we? Will we?

What Can Be Done

F: I think that's up to the two of you. You're smart, you care about Centerville, you have influence, and you have proven over the years that you're both good leaders. Plus, your organizations have given you the power to make decisions here today. Are there any reasons you <u>can't</u> do these things?

W: I guess not.

K: If we commit ourselves and work together, we can do it.

(NOTE: The gradual development of "Power-WITH" has been going on from the very beginning of the meeting, and now has firmly established itself as the kind of power essential to moving forward effectively.)

How To Do It

In one sense, the final part of LifeSkill #5, How To Do It, has been on-going. Using the LifeSkills is an effective way "to do it", whatever the "it" might be, and Fran, Walt and Kris have been using all the LifeSkills at their meeting.

*(NOTE: The "How To Do It" portion of LifeSkill #5 flows seamlessly into LifeSkill #6 (Focus on Process and Develop "Doables"). Indeed, LifeSkill #6 is a major part of "How To Do It")

We will discuss #6 thoroughly in the next chapter, but I don't want to leave the Centerville case hanging. So we will look at a bit more of the meeting, realizing that these concluding entries flow seamlessly into LifeSkill #6.

F: Okay then, what could be a good first step? *(Fran is asking for a "Doable", a very feasible step that can build momentum, trust, and a foundation for additional, bigger steps.)*

K: We can make a joint public statement committing ourselves and our organizations to finding a good location for a shopping mall other than the park. And SOCK will help in finding such a place.

W: That's a good step, but I think we should meet with our organizations before that and explain our agreements. We don't want them to first hear about it on TV or in the newspaper.

F: Who will do what by when?

K: Walt, let's get together after this meeting and draft our joint statement. Then we each call a meeting of our organizations, get their commitment, and after that we call the newspaper and TV station. Fran? I think you should appear on TV with us.

W: I agree. (Fran also agrees.)

The outcomes of the Centerville case? Here they are.

A large parcel of vacant land owned by the town was chosen as the site for the small shopping mall. An adjoining piece of vacant land was bought by the town to provide ample parking space for mall shoppers.

The SOCK and BOP organizations transformed and renamed themselves, SOCK becoming the Community Environmental Center, and BOP becoming the Progressive Business Group. They all agreed CEC and PBG were much better than SOCK and BOP.

Concluding Remarks

The NCH LifeSkill is really quite obvious and logical. Then why do we so often ignore or violate it? I suggest there are several reasons.

One, we do not perceive it as a Skill. Treating it as a practical and important Skill with a specific name helps us remember it and use it.

Two, as already discussed, we do not differentiate between needs and desires. Far too often we convince ourselves if we want something, we "need" it.

Three, we forget to focus on the practical "who does what by when", thereby ignoring the steps needed to make our actions and interactions effective.

Four, we often *focus on desired outcomes and do not develop an effective Process*. That important understanding constitutes LifeSkill #6, to which we now turn.

Chapter 6

LifeSkill #6: Focus on a Quality Process To Produce Effective Outcomes

*Life itself
and all therein
is a journey unfolding,
discovery awaiting....*
    *A journey of moments,
of falling and rising
of knowing and searching
of Being and Becoming......*
        *A journey of steps
each holding worth,
teaching us where
the next step can be.......*
            *And the place we arrive
is where we should be
if we learned from the steps
along the way.*

All the LifeSkills discussed thus far work together as critical steps in building a process to accomplish any endeavor with quality. The specifics presented in LifeSkill #6 complete the process.

Outline of Chapter 6
1. Exploring the Ingredients of "Process"
2. Effective Options
3. "Doables"
4. The Three W's
5. Mutual Benefit Outcomes that are Sustainable

1. Exploring the Ingredients of "Process"
Effective outcomes emerge from effective Process.

Even though this important understanding has proven itself to be true time and time again, far too often we ignore or pay inadequate attention to Process. We focus primarily on preconceived outcomes, and either try to leap to those outcomes or take the most convenient short cut. In doing so, we (1) miss the valuable lessons of "discovery" along the way; and (2) often end up with outcomes that are faulty and/or unsustainable.

If you will, picture this scene. Two good friends, Alan and Trish, decide to go on a hiking trip to a place neither has previously visited. Before leaving the city, they briefly consult a map. All it shows is a meadow nestled between two mountain ridges. The meadow is called Ram's Field, so named because many mountain goats live there. There's only one way to reach the meadow by foot. Climb up to one of the ridges, cross it, and descend to the meadow below.

Alan and Trish decide to have some competitive fun. He will start at the base of one ridge, she will start at the base of the other ridge, and they will race to see who gets to Ram's Field first. The one who gets there last has to buy the winner a fancy dinner.

They leave the city early on a Saturday morning. Alan drops Trish off at the foot of her ridge, then drives to the foot of his ridge. Being the more experienced and accomplished hiker, Alan is full of confidence. He looks at the distant ridge, sees a slight gap, and decides that's the best place to cross.

Keeping his eyes fixated on the gap, he charges boldly ahead. He does not notice the numerous tracks of mountain goats, all of which are headed in a different direction than his preconceived route.

After two hours, he reaches the gap. He has made excellent time and is certain he will handily beat Trish to the meadow.

Suddenly, his confidence plummets as he sees his preconceived place to cross over the ridge is a deep gorge. It stretches far to his left and his right, making it impossible to cross anywhere near his present position. Cursing and blaming his predicament on "bad luck", he expends valuable time and energy searching for a way to cross the ridge.

Alan's predicament was not due to "bad luck", of course. It was due to his stubborn fixation on what seemed from afar to be the best crossing spot (the gap), and his lack of a flexible Process within which he could learn from the steps along the way.

Meanwhile, Trish was doing much better. From the very beginning of her climb up the unfamiliar terrain, she focused on a Process: to look for signs along the way that might indicate the best place to cross the ridge. When she saw the tracks of the mountain goats, she followed them. After all, the meadow was named Ram's Field for a reason. Mountain goats lived there. Surely they knew the best way to get home from their excursions in the mountains.

Trish easily crossed the ridge and climbed down to the meadow. Alan finally arrived an hour later.

Pride, bragging rights among their hiker friends, earning a fancy dinner.....those were the not-so-important stakes in the Alan and Trish example. Many of the situations we are involved in each day have far greater stakes. The principle, however, is the same. *Effective outcomes emerge from effective Process.*

A "Process" is a pathway of steps that provides direction, a journey that blends........
- Goals
- Wise and creative planning
- Specific skills
- The flexibility to learn from steps along the way
- The capacity to use that learning to make needed adjustments
- Ethics

Goals and desired outcomes as originally designed are not sacred or set in concrete. An effective Process helps us learn if the objectives we originally set should be maintained as they are, revised slightly, or changed significantly.

The first steps in an effective Process should be chosen carefully, for they set us on a particular direction. Each and every subsequent step should help us discover what the next steps should be, make needed changes in prior plans, and build confidence and momentum. Outcomes become the culmination of a Process.

All of the LifeSkills we are discussing in this book provide practical, hands-on tools in the development and implementation of an effective process. When we weave the LifeSkills with other important principles, we emerge with a set of handy guidelines for developing an effective, quality Process.

Guidelines for Developing an Effective Process
    1. Consider the **Broader Context** in which the Process will take place. (Refer back to Chapter 1.)
    2. What are the **needs and goals** the Process will be designed to accomplish?
    3. What **resources** are needed to make the Process work? Do we currently have access to those resources? If not, can they realistically be obtained? How? Are we the ones who are most capable of designing and implementing the Process? (This guideline relates to the "Focus on What **Can** Be Done" portion of the NCH LifeSkill.)
    4. Seek **input** in design and implementation from **the parties who will be affected** by the Process.
    5. **Match tasks with capabilities**. If existing personnel do not have the necessary capabilities to make the Process work, either provide training or re-examine whether or not the task is actually needed.
    6. Choose the **first steps** in the Process based on the following criteria:
        (a) They are extremely feasible.
        (b) They involve at least some participation by the parties whose support will be needed to make the Process work.
        (c) They clearly lead and are connected to following steps that are more substantive and complex.
        (d) They generate enthusiasm, momentum, and support for the Process.
        (e) They are designed with the "who does what by when" principle clearly evident.
    7. Allow the Process to "**unfold**", don't make it too rigid. In other words, we need to **learn from each step,** and, based on what we

learn, make needed alterations to any original plan.

8. Give continuous attention to the **ethics** of the Process. *The means we use to accomplish an outcome say as much about our quality as individuals and groups as does the outcome itself.*

9. Build in **regular assessments** and use the assessments to make any needed changes.

10. Throughout the process, **continue using all of the LifeSkills.**

11. Keep generating **effective options** throughout planning and implementation.

2. Generate Effective Options

Generating Options gives us more choices. Most people agree with that simple fact, yet often do an inadequate job of generating options. Why? Here are a few explanations.

- The "my way is the only way" pattern takes over.
- The Broader Context of situations is ignored, thereby limiting the range of options.
- Rigid preconceived "answers" make generating other options seem unnecessary.
- "Demands" are perceived by the party issuing the demands as being the same as "options". However, because they are stated as demands, the other sees them as rigid, take-it-or-leave-it pronouncements, not as options open to constructive dialogue.

Before getting to what makes an option effective, a brief comment on "Brainstorming" seems appropriate. The goal of brainstorming is to open the mind and start the creative juices flowing. Some of the brainstormed options may not be very realistic, and might even be received with a rolling of the eyes, or humor. And that's okay. At least the optioning process has begun.

Obviously, generating **effective** options is more important and more difficult. Here are a few criteria for what makes an option <u>effective</u>.

Criteria for What Makes an Option Effective

1. The option <u>can be done</u> by all parties involved in a situation.

2. The option meets an Individual and/or Shared Need.

3. The parties who affect and are affected by the option have some input in shaping and implementing the option.

4. The implementation of the option does not depend on

outside actors or forces with whom the actual parties involved in an interaction have little or no influence.

5. Within interactions, accomplishing the option utilizes Power-WITH.

6. The option will result in <u>mutual benefits</u>, and does not give advantage to one party over the other.

7. The values and ethics that will be used to accomplish the option are consistent with the values and goals of the intended outcome.

8. The option has the built-in possibility to lead to other effective options.

There are several guidelines for generating effective options.

Guidelines for Generating Effective Options

- **Focus on potential possibilities before looking at potential obstacles.**

To be sure, the difficulties facing any task need to be identified and understood as a step in the process of accomplishing the task. Yet, if we begin with a focus on why we think we <u>cannot</u> do something, we often create an atmosphere that weakens our search for what we <u>can</u> do.

We need to look at the needs, the resources required to meet those needs, and at least a few options <u>before</u> we consider the potential obstacles. The LifeSkill, Generate Effective Options, helps direct energy toward the creation of *possibilities*. Some of the things we would have initially considered obstacles fade away because we now have a clearer vision of potential steps we can take.

- **Focus on "proposals" rather than "demands".**

As previously mentioned, Demands (1) almost always influence the other party to feel defensive; (2) are usually impossible for the other party to do because the demands are purposely designed to give the demanding party the advantage; and (3) often express desires rather than needs. Offering "proposals" is much more effective than issuing "demands", especially if the proposals are designed to produce <u>mutual</u> benefits. They become more powerful and much more likely to be adopted and implemented.

- **Try to generate options that (a) are based on Individual and Shared Needs; (b) utilize "Power-WITH"; and (c) can actually be done by the other party.**

- **Try to generate options together with the other party, and give the other party a chance to suggest an option first.**

Now let's look at an example of Generating Effective Options.

Example A: The Apartment

Cindy and Miki, two twenty-something women from different parts of the country, recently graduated from their respective medical schools. Upon graduation, they were both invited into the intern program at a large medical center in another part of the country. In searching for apartments, they met each other, and decided to become apartment mates. That was one month ago. They have already discovered just how different they are.

Cindy is quiet, shy, rarely socializes, and has to put in long hours of study to keep up with the other interns. Miki is vivacious, socializes a lot, and is so adept academically she has to study about half as much as Cindy.

Miki frequently entertains friends at the apartment, sometimes long into the night. Cindy usually stays in her room trying to study, but the noise from Miki's parties makes concentration difficult. Miki is always telling Cindy, "You should come join us. Being a good doctor involves getting along with people, not just knowing facts from books."

Cindy knows she should confront Miki about how her life style is causing problems in their shared living space. But Cindy has always avoided dealing with conflicts. To her, conflicts are like ugly pimples on what should be the smooth complexion of life. She believes nice and intelligent people shouldn't have conflicts. So she avoids dealing with the situation for at least a month.

Finally, Miki suggests they go to a nice restaurant for dinner to "talk about how our being apartment mates is going". Cindy nervously agrees. During dinner, the following conversation takes place. (M=Miki, C=Cindy)

M: I really like you, Cindy. You're one of the nicest people I've ever known. But I think you have problems with me and my personality.
C: I...I like you, too.
M: Thanks. But I think you have problems with me. Right?
C: It's....well....it's hard to study sometimes when you have your parties.
M: It's your apartment, too, so let's figure out some options for how to make it better. Any suggestions?

C: I...I guess I could go to the library every night and study there.
M: That's what I thought you would suggest. Do you think that's a good option?
C: (pause) It's the only one I can think of right now.
M: Let's think of some other options. Like...I could stop having friends over. Or I could invite only those friends who are so quiet they seem comatose. Or we could alternate nights being in charge of what happens at the apartment. Or one of us could move out. Or you could party more. Do you like any of those options? You think any of them will actually work?

*(*Break: *Do you readers think any of the options generated thus far are "effective" options? If so, why? If not, why not?)*

Now back to the Miki-Cindy conversation.
C: Do I like any of those options? Not really.
M: I don't like them either. I was just brainstorming ideas to get us started.
C: I don't want to argue about it. I really dislike arguments. So maybe I should go to the library like I suggested.
M: Stand up for yourself, Cindy. I make it hard for you to study so you have to go to the library? That place is like a dungeon, and usually too hot or too cold. If we do that option you'd be the only one making adjustments. That's not fair.
C: I.... I appreciate what you're saying, and I'm glad we had a dinner out together. But I should get back to the apartment. I have a lot of studying to finish tonight.
M: (grinning) If I have to chain you to this table until we decide on something, I'll do it. Now tell me what you need in our living situation, I'll tell you what I need, and we'll see what needs are the same. Then we'll come up with what to do.
C: Well....okay. What do I need? I need to study more than you do. You're naturally brilliant, I'm not. And I guess I need to be a bit more social, but it's not natural for me, and when I see all the friends you have, it makes me feel.....I guess it makes me feel even more introverted.
M: Let me see if I understand. I heard you saying you need to study more, and you feel like you should be more social but it's not a natural thing for you. Is that what you meant?"
C: Yes.

M: Okay, my turn. What do I need? I need for us to have more time together. I need a close friend I can talk with. Most of my other friends just like to have a good time. It gets too shallow sometimes. And...what do you think we both need? You know....the same needs?

C: To feel comfortable where we live...and to be prepared for the next day at the hospital.... and, like you, I need a friend I feel comfortable talking about things with. This is a very stressful, demanding, and important time in our lives.

M: I agree those are things we both need. So....what do we do to meet your needs, my needs, and our shared needs? Maybe not all of them, but the most important ones.

C: Maybe you can give me more advance notice before inviting a group of friends over.

M: Definitely. And I don't need to have people over so often. If truth be known, I would prefer to go to a movie a couple of times a month with you and a couple of friends. And I would also like for us to go out to dinner together regularly and just talk. Like we're doing now. Which reminds me. I've been wanting to get your advice about how to deal with Dr. Buford. You seem to get along with her better than the rest of us do.

C: And I want to get your advice on James, that guy you introduced me to last week. He asked me out on a date....but I think he's dating Cheryl.

M: Hmmm. Interesting. Here's what I know about James.

(They talk for another thirty minutes, then walk home. Because they have generated some effective options, they have made a good start on improving life at the apartment.) Why are the options Miki and Cindy developed "effective" options?

(1) They meet individual and shared needs.
(2) Neither of the women is disadvantaged by the options. Rather, both Miki and Cindy benefit.
(3) The options are feasible.
(4) The options are generated by both of the women (they use Power-WITH).
(5) The options will lead to other options now that Miki nd Cindy are feeling more comfortable with each other and are communicating well.

After Generating Options, What's the Next Step?
After generating effective options, we need to decide what to do next. It is at this point we sometimes stumble and have difficulty solving problems, resolving conflicts, or making and implementing effective plans. One of the reasons is that we choose as the next step an option that is too big. We focus on the "grand designs" of the outcome, rather than building a "pathway of steppingstones". I call these steppingstones "Doables".

3. Develop "Doables"
What Are "Doables"?
Picture a Process as being a pathway. *Doables are "steppingstones" that help build that pathway. They are action steps on smaller issues and tasks, not on the larger, more difficult, or more conflictual issues.*
What "Doables" Accomplish
Doables.........
- Provide a safe, feasible first step that shows constructive action is possible.
- Provide an initial success on which trust, confidence and momentum can be developed.
- Provide an effective alternative to the ineffective pattern of trying to do too much too soon, a pattern than usually ends in failure and discouragement.
- Each Doable helps shed light on what the next Doable should be.

Summarizing the Characteristics of Effective Doables
An effective Doable.......
1. Is an action step dealing with a smaller issue or task, not something bigger, more contentious, or more difficult.
2. Is feasible. It can be done, it is "able to be done".
3. Can be accomplished <u>through the efforts of the parties involved in the interaction, task, and/or conflict</u>. The most effective Doables do not depend on the decisions and actions of an outside party with whom the actual participants have no influence.
4. Can be accomplished with the resources already in the hands of the parties involved, or with additional resources that can be obtained. In other words, make sure the needed resources will be available or else the action will not be "doable".

5. Results in <u>mutual</u> benefits, and utilizes "<u>Power-WITH</u>". (NOTE: Some Doables may be "trust-building steps" taken by each party. In other words, each party voluntarily does something individually to show trustworthiness and a commitment to constructive progress. However, those individual Doables are not enough. Doables producing <u>mutual</u> benefits must also be developed and implemented.)

6. Leads to other Doables and to the eventual accomplishment of larger and more difficult tasks and agreements.

7. Uses behavior and ethics that are consistent with the values and ethics underlying the intended outcome of the Doable.

I am sure you have thought of examples from your own experiences demonstrating how Doables either played or perhaps should have played an important role. Here are two examples from my experiences.

Example B: The Divided Community

This example comes from a situation I worked in several years ago in an urban community beset with many problems. Racial and youth gang violence, unemployment, pollution, lack of health care (the hospitals had moved to the suburbs to escape the vandalism and violence)....these were but a few of the problems.

I finally managed to arrange a meeting with five of the most influential leaders of the community. They knew they had to begin working together or else their community would split apart, damaging <u>all</u> of the sectors of the community. But nobody had taken the lead.

Those present at the meeting were: (1) the president of the community's small business association; (2) the head of the Town Council; (3) the president of the school board; (4) the managing editor of the community newspaper, who was also on the Board of the major TV station; and (5) a youth counselor who had been in a gang and still had good contacts with gang members.

It was the first time all of them had met together. During the past few months, their main interaction was blaming each other for many of the community problems. They sat in the room silently, not one of them feeling enough trust or potential cooperation to initiate dialogue.

The process I decided to try began with inviting them to focus on what <u>connected</u> them, not just on what divided them. I asked them to do something individually: to write down on a piece of paper eight major <u>needs of the community</u>. They clearly thought it was a useless exercise, but reluctantly did it, none of them wanting to appear "obstructionist".

Next, I took the pieces of paper and looked for Shared Needs. I found three needs listed by all of the five leaders. Rather than telling them what I found, I asked if they thought there were any needs appearing on all of the pieces of paper. They did not seem very interested in answering the question.

As is true in most conflict situations, Shared Needs do exist even though the conflict parties are not looking for them. I went ahead and told them what the three shared needs were. I suggested they talk about those three needs to see if action might be taken on any of them. After a period of resistance, they were finally willing to offer a few comments.

One of the shared needs was job training for teenagers and young adults. Everybody felt job opportunities would help get the youth off the streets and be less tempted to join violent gangs.

A second shared need was a community-wide project to improve the antiquated sewer system while also resurfacing the cracked and potholed streets.

There was a third need all the leaders had identified, which I'll mention in a minute.

I asked which of the three shared needs they thought was most important, and they said either the job training or improving the sewer system. When I asked if they were willing to work together on one of those, they all said there wasn't enough trust in the community to do the job training, and the public works project was too expensive and too massive. They said trying either of those two ideas would result in certain failure, which would further depress the community.

It was a perfect time for a Doable, something that was needed, was small enough to accomplish, and would be a first step in showing the leaders they could indeed cooperate.

The third shared need became the Doable. What was it? Putting more street lights throughout the community. For whatever reasons, the community had the fewest street lights of any town its size I had ever seen. The darkness made people afraid to go outside at night because of the youth gangs, which also led to people staying in their homes rather than getting together for evening social events that could have helped improve community relations.

"What about this Shared Need?" I asked. "What would it take to get street lights?"

One of them answered, "We would all have to sign a petition, all of us as community leaders, and have the Town Council present it to the larger municipality who is responsible for such things."

"Well," I encouraged, "who wants to sign first?"

There was dead silence. I could feel their brains working. They were realizing that a Doable had emerged, something they could not ignore by saying it was "impossible", or took too long to implement, or would fail and make them look bad as leaders. Obtaining more street lights was imminently feasible and would benefit everybody. It was a first step they could cooperate on together and show good leadership.

Finally, the editor of the newspaper suggested we take a fifteen minute break during which she would draft the petition. After the break, the other leaders approved the draft, it was typed and printed, and they all signed it.

It took only a month for the street lights to be installed. The impasse and the assumption the five leaders could not work together disappeared because of the Doable. It helped them realize they needed each other, they could use Power-WITH without losing their personal power, and they could move on to larger projects the community needed.

Within five months the job training program was underway. The municipal government, impressed with the new-found cooperation, allocated start-up funding for the sewer system project.

The Doable, by itself, did not solve all their problems or resolve all their conflicts. But it was a critical step in opening up possibilities, it was a "steppingstone" in the process of improving the quality of community life.

Example C: In the Aftermath

This example takes place in a country where a three-month ethnic civil war resulted in a shockingly high number of brutal deaths. Although the international community had done little to prevent the carnage, several nations jumped in during the month after the killing had stopped.

The development agency from one of the nations predetermined what was needed to restore some semblance of peace to the frightened and shocked people who had just gone through the civil war. The agency decided seminars on "Respecting Human Rights" should be conducted at fifteen sites throughout the ravaged country. The seminars were advertised, experts from around the world were brought in to speak on human rights.....and out of the total population of the country only twenty citizens showed up at the seminars!

The agency was dismayed. I was called in as a consultant, and asked the leaders of the agency, "Did you consult the people themselves on what they felt would be a good program to offer?"

"They need to develop respect for human rights," was the adamant reply. "They slaughtered each other, hundreds-of-thousands! Why? Because they don't respect each other's basic human rights!"

"Why do you think only twenty people showed up for your seminars on human rights?" I asked.

The agency leaders debated several possible reasons for the lack of attendance, but never considered the most important one. Trying to get the ethnic groups to focus on human rights so soon after the horrible war was too big, too volatile. The seminars would become a new battleground as each group blamed the other for violating "my" human rights.

So holding seminars wasn't the problem. Providing an opportunity for members of the two ethnic groups to come together for a shared experience was a constructive idea. The problem was the content of the seminars and their timing. So soon after the war, the content needed to focus on a less threatening topic than human rights and how those rights were violated in the war. Those seminars could be effective later. In other words, human rights seminars were not "doable" at that particular time, as clearly evidenced by the lack of attendance.

I explained the concept of Doables, then said, "Your agency is good at conducting seminars, you do it all over the world. What is a more feasible topic than human rights, something they all want to learn? It might serve as a first step in showing they can be in the same place at the same time without using violence. Dealing directly with human rights might be more possible later after the Doable has succeeded."

The agency, to its credit, went back to the drawing board. They sent a team to spend two weeks talking to citizens from both ethnic groups. The comments from the citizens revealed several Shared Needs and educational interests. A Doable that would bring members of both ethnic groups together at seminars across the country began to emerge. It would provide a small but essential first step in giving the two groups a chance to sit side by side as fellow "learners" of skills they both wanted and needed. *They would not be sitting next to each other as ethnic enemies.*

And what was the Doable? Seminars on computer training.

"Huh?!" you might be saying. "Computer training?! An incredible number of people were slaughtered, and you want to have computer training seminars?!" But look what happened.

The fifteen sites couldn't accommodate all of the people who came. As they sat side by side, ethnic and war enemies four months ago, they began talking about what key to hit on the computer as the lessons progressed, and at the breaks, they gradually began sharing their shock at what they had allowed to happen in the country they both loved. Within another four months, enough people were ready to start discussing, from the heart, the need for mutual respect regardless of ethnicity, and to focus on taking specific steps to build that mutual respect. They themselves organized all the steps as the process emerged.

The Doable of computer seminars had nothing to do with the causes of the civil war. But the seminars, because they were non-threatening and focused on an expressed Shared Need and educational interest, was the first step in bringing the two ethnic groups together in the same place for something other than fighting. And that's what Doables can accomplish. They can "break the impasse", they can "be a steppingstone in beginning a process", they can make it possible to begin a pathway to the accomplishment of larger, more difficult tasks.

(NOTE: Although the international agency organized the initial seminars, the citizens themselves took charge of the actual reconciliation efforts.....and made them work.)

4. The Three W's: Who Does What by When

As was pointed out in our discussion of the NCH LifeSkill, some of the elements that constitute a successful process are taken for granted. We assume they are being implemented, but in actuality they are not. They fall between the cracks and weaken the process. This is one of the many reasons why having a set of practical skills and principles, each one with a name we can readily remember, enhances our effectiveness.

One of those named Skills is what I call The Three W's: Who Does What by When. A process will not be effective unless this skill is actually perceived as a skill deserving our attention and action.

In implementing the Three W's, I suggest there are three key guidelines that need to be followed.

- **Match the "Who" and the "What".** A task (the "What") needs to be matched with the person (the "Who") most capable of completing the task with quality. Sometimes this seemingly obvious guideline is not followed. Why? The reasons vary depending on the situation.

Let's say a particular task needs to be done, and an enthusiastic volunteer steps forward. Enthusiastic volunteerism is noble, of course, and deserves support. Yet, we need to find out if that particular volunteer has the skills to do the task effectively. We need to match the "who" with the "what".

Another reason might be faulty job descriptions. The description is so vague nobody is quite sure who is supposed to do what. "I didn't know that was my responsibility" is a frequent response, or "I thought (so-and-so) was supposed to do that."

A third possible reason why the What and the Who are not matched very well is pride. A person is given a task, knows he/she lacks the skills to do it well, but does not want to admit , "I'm not the best person for that particular task, I think (so-and-so) is more qualified."

- **Use Wisdom in Determining the "When".** There are some situations where firm deadlines for completing a task cannot be altered. Even in those cases we need to reexamine the deadlines to make sure they are feasible. Completing a task with thoroughness and quality is more important than simply "getting it done" in order to stick with an unrealistic due-date. The outcome will be inadequate and probably require going back and re-doing some things, thereby taking even more time than if the deadline had been extended.

- **Build In Clear Accountability and Assessment Along the Way.** Accountability (Who is responsible for What by When) needs to be crystal clear from the very beginning of a process. Assessment (evaluation of how well a task is being done) needs to occur regularly as the process moves along, not put off until the process has been completed.

5. Develop Mutual Benefit Outcomes and Make Them Sustainable

The final part of LifeSkill #6 reminds us once again of the critical principle, *Effective outcomes emerge from effective Process*. If we build and implement a quality process, we stand an excellent chance of producing quality outcomes.

Two of the important characteristics of quality outcomes are (a) they contain mutual benefits for all the parties involved; and (b) they are sustainable.

Why Mutual Benefit Outcomes Are Important

Experience teaches us that the quality and success of relationships and interactions are greatly enhanced when all the parties involved benefit from the relationship or interaction. Each party both receives and contributes; each party feels greater commitment; the power becomes Power-WITH rather than a competition for power-over; and sustaining the outcomes becomes a shared goal.

With such obvious incentives for promoting <u>mutual</u> benefits, one might wonder why their attainment is often ignored and even obstructed.

Why Mutual Benefits Are Not Attained
Interpretations of "Dominance"

Some people seem to believe humans are programmed to seek dominance over each other when given the slightest opportunity. Seeking dominance in relationships and interactions is seen as "human nature", a kind of social manifestation of Darwin's Survival of the Fittest theories. Some people even argue that the only way to feel "secure" and "powerful" is to gain a position of dominance over others. Furthermore, there are other people who seem to believe a dominance hierarchy is essential to create and maintain "order" in relationships, interactions, and society as a whole.

I contend some of those interpretations of dominance are myths, and others are short-sighted. Here are my reasons.

• As a relatively young species with most of our potential yet to be discovered and developed, our "human nature" is a work in progress. Within our "nature" as humans, there is a vast array of behaviors we choose from every day. They are all components of human nature. To be sure, dominance is one, but so is cooperation and seeking mutual benefits. In other words, we as humans are not programmed to choose dominance.

• Dominance usually produces damaging conflicts that negatively affect both the dominated and the dominator. In dealing with the conflict, the dominator usually continues to use domination, further worsening the situation for all concerned.

• Dominance creates insecurity in the one being dominated, which in turn makes the relationship or interaction less secure and effective. As discussed in LifeSkill #3, each party is more secure if all parties are secure, so even the dominator eventually becomes less secure.

• Dominance obstructs the other party's contributions and full participation, which in turn diminishes the potential of any relationship, interaction, task and process. Clearly, the one being dominated is denied the opportunity to contribute fully, but the dominator is denied something, too; namely, the benefits that could come from the other party's contributions.

- Gaining dominance and Power-Over creates "enemies". Valuable time, energy and resources are diverted from constructive aspects of a relationship or interaction as the dominator focuses on defending and protecting the position of dominance.

The Pattern of "Social Profit"

Another reason why mutual benefit outcomes are not realized is what I call "Social Profit". This pattern has its roots in economics, especially in those societies, systems and theories in which economic success is defined by profit margins.

At its generic root, "profit" means getting more out of something then is put in. I suggest the notion of profit in economic terms is so unquestioned and pervasive, it has been subconsciously transferred to apply to the social aspects of life. Getting more out of a relationship or interaction than is put in becomes almost a habit for many people. The critical importance of mutual benefit outcomes is obscured by the Social Profit pattern.

The Ecstacy of "Winning" and the Agony of Losing

Volumes have been written on "competition", some extolling its virtues as the primary engine of progress, others deploring its dearth of ethics. I would like to focus on the aspect of competition that worships "winning" and abhors "losing", the notion that the only real purpose of competition is to win, and losing is a tragedy.

As an avid sports enthusiast, I felt compelled years ago to write about "Sudden Death", the terminology used in American football. As football fans know, the term refers to the overtime period if the score is tied at the end of regulation time. The first team that scores wins the game.

In my writings, I pointed out the obvious: the term Sudden Death conveys the notion that losing is so bad it's like dying. A lot of people commented (sometimes good-naturedly) that I was being ridiculous, that I was reading way too much into an innocent choice of words chosen to increase drama. My reply, "Language reflects culture", was considered by some football enthusiasts as three wasted words that had nothing to do with athletics.

Moving along, I think the point is clear. Winning can be elevated to such heights that the only level left for losing is rock bottom, and, sometimes, keeping from losing can become almost as much an obsession as winning.

Lost in the competition is the value of _mutual_ benefits, and the reality that nobody really loses when mutual benefits are the outcomes of a relationship or interaction.

I guess most of us enjoy winning. I would like to believe the reason is because we know we performed well and accomplished a goal, not because the competitor lost.

(Side Note: Somewhat recently, many athletic programs, especially involving younger athletes, have decided to stop using the term Sudden Death. The creative and welcomed search for alternative terminology will again demonstrate, "Language reflects culture".)

A Process Involving Proven Skills is Not Implemented

It is stating the obvious to say once again that mutual benefit outcomes will not magically appear just because we want them and consider them important. They occur in relationships and interactions through the use of specific attitudes and skills.

All of the six LifeSkills we have been discussing throughout this book apply directly to the development and realization of mutual benefit outcomes. Ignoring any one of the LifeSkills will be detrimental to the process producing the outcomes and to the outcomes themselves. As we have seen, the LifeSkills work together to strengthen each other. They constitute a process that gives us the best chance of producing _mutual_ benefits.

The LifeSkills also help make the outcomes _sustainable_, the final topic of this chapter.

Building Sustainability

Mutual benefit outcomes need to be sustainable, they need to last. Using all of the LifeSkills help build sustainability, so we have already done some of the work. There are a couple of points I would like to reemphasize, and a few additional suggestions I would like to offer. A specific case will be used to highlight these points.

The case involves a new department supervisor, appointed a month ago, and the eight employees he manages. The month has not gone well, and poor supervisor-employee communication is a major reason. They blame each other for the problem. Frustrated and confused, the supervisor finally convenes an all-day departmental meeting. By the end of the day, everyone feels a good outcome has resulted.

Within two weeks, the old problems return. The outcome of the meeting has not proven sustainable. Let's look at several key principles that, if implemented, could have promoted sustainability.

- **Participation helps promote sustainability.**

People tend to work more diligently to make an outcome sustainable if they have a role in shaping and implementing the process that produces the outcome. Although the supervisor was well-intentioned and had some good ideas, he did not create a process that invited suggestions from the employees before giving his own.

- **The Three W's go hand in hand with sustainability.**

Building into an outcome a clear understanding and schedule of Who Does What by When promotes effective sustainability. Clear job and task descriptions are part of The Three W's. Although a number of departmental changes were identified and approved, who was to do what by when was left unclear. The supervisor assumed each employee understood his or her role in the changes, but that was not the case. The employees did not want to appear "dumb" so didn't clarify The Three W's or point out why the new job descriptions were confusing. Furthermore, the few specific assignments that were given by the supervisor did not match personnel with skills. The employees who were assigned certain tasks were the least qualified to complete those particular tasks with quality.

- **Built-in follow-up promotes sustainability.**

Even if we think an outcome is so solid it does not need follow up steps, build them in anyway. On the surface, the day-long meeting seemed successful. But nobody thought to suggest a simple, practical follow-up: weekly, Monday morning meetings of the entire staff to plan the week and to reinforce a pattern of constructive communication.

- **On-going assessments are crucial in making outcomes sustainable.**

Outcomes are living, breathing accomplishments that need to be evaluated as they unfold, and if the assessments identify needed alterations, they should be made. Thankful at last to have had a meeting and produce what seemed to be a good outcome, nobody thought on-going assessments were needed. (They are always needed no matter how confident we are in the outcomes we have produced.)

- **Attending to structural and systemic factors is essential to making an outcome effective and sustainable.**

Outcomes do not exist within a vacuum; they are influenced by whatever structural and systemic conditions surround them. Those structures and systems are part of the Broader Context, the "Circle".

Some outcomes can be sustained in certain structures and systems but not in others. We may be able to produce the outcomes, but we are not always able to influence some of the structures and systems in which those outcomes must exist.

Applying LifeSkill #1, Focus on the Broader Context, at the very beginning of a process helps us identify the structures we must operate within, which we can influence, and which we cannot. Waiting until the process has yielded outcomes may be too late, causing the outcomes to be unsustainable. I suggest we should work hard to influence the structures, but sometimes they are so dominant and established they are basically immune to alteration.

In the example we are using, the supervisor and employees did not take into account a very important structure in the company as a whole. A newly established policy required every "major" change in a department's operating procedures to be pre-approved by the company's CEO. The supervisor did not consider the departmental changes "major" enough to fall under the policy.

The CEO learned of the changes a week after they had been implemented. He was furious at the supervisor for failing to adhere to the policy. Although the CEO found nothing wrong with the content of the changes, he felt he had to (a) assert his authority, and (b) maintain consistency throughout the company by strictly enforcing the new policy.

The result? The CEO disallowed two of the changes that were outcomes of the supervisor-employees meeting. Those particular changes were linked to other changes, so the fledgling progress the department had made fell like a stack of cards.

If the supervisor and/or employees had paid attention to and clarified an important part of the company decision-making *structure* (the new policy), the CEO would have readily approved the changes.

Transition from Part I to Part II

Part I has presented the six LifeSkills.
Focus on the Broader Context
Focus on Connections
Develop Secure Self, Secure Other, Secure We
Clarify
Focus on NCH (What Needs To Be Done, Can Be Done, and How To Do It)
Focus on a Quality Process to Produce Effective Outcomes

These critical LifeSkills enrich the quality and effectiveness of any endeavor, any relationship, any interaction. Many diverse examples have already been provided. Part II presents three more actual cases in greater depth.

Part II
Actual Cases

Chapter 7: The Toy Company

Janet Taylor was the only child in a poor but loving family. When she was seventeen, her parents died in an automobile accident. With no relatives capable of helping her, Janet was on her own. Intelligent, resourceful and a hard worker, she applied to a good university and was accepted. She was awarded a partial scholarship but still had to work at various jobs to make ends meet. She graduated when she was twenty-two.

Completely on her own, Janet needed a job as quickly as possible. The job market was so tight she had to spend the next four months searching for employment. She finally stumbled on a company called Toy Universe (TU), specializing in the manufacture and sale of a wide assortment of children's toys. She was offered a job after only one interview, and eagerly grabbed the opportunity.

Janet knew next to nothing about TU, but believed her skills could contribute significantly to any company. She had majored in business in college, made excellent grades, and possessed strong relationship skills. The job she was offered was in the Client Relations Department, headed by a man named Glen Smathers who would be her immediate boss. Her position was called Client Relations Liaison (CRL), and she was one of only three CRL's at the company. Her duties consisted of establishing and maintaining good relations with the toy stores selling TU products.

On the surface, the job seemed to be a perfect match with Janet's skills. And it was, except for one thing. After only a few days on the job, she discovered that forty percent of the toys the company produced and sold fell into her definition of "violent" toys.

There were toy weapons that looked so real a careless military procurement chief might buy them for his troops.

There were sets of battery-powered toys pitting evil monsters against heroes in a battle to the death. (An accompanying repair kit cost extra.)

And there were toys that seemed to promote a subtle message of sexist and racist stereotypes, which Janet saw as a form of nonphysical violence but violence just the same.

She was faced with a dilemma. She had always believed violent toys make no constructive contribution to human society, numb children to the horrors of violence, and make using guns more acceptable to those children when they become adults. And here she was working for a company that had 40% of its sales in violent toys. She felt she was compromising one of her values.

During her first month on the job, Janet was so busy just doing her job she didn't have much time to think about her dilemma. It remained with her, however, and her frustration increased. She was angry with herself for not doing more research on TU before so quickly accepting the job offer. But that was the past. She had to focus on the present and the immediate future. She decided she had to take action before her frustration got even worse.

(**NOTE: We will go through Janet's next few days with her. Her use of the LifeSkills will be highlighted, as will those incidents when she could have used a particular LifeSkill but did not.**)

Janet wisely decided the first step was to look at the "complete picture", the components of her overall situation. In other words, she applied **LifeSkill #1, Focus on the Broader Context**, and identified the components in the Circle. Here's what the complete picture looked like to her.

• She wanted to keep her values as intact as possible.
• She was barely making ends meet so needed to keep her job. Finding alternative employment, if even possible, would take far too long.
• A lot of her job was indeed perfect for her, and, after all, if 40% of the toys were violent, that meant 60% of the toys were in keeping with her values.
• From what she could tell, the people running the company had never been challenged to think about the violent toy issue.
• Glen, her immediate boss, seemed to be a nice man, had three children of his own, and consistently praised Janet's job performance.
• The company's priority was maximizing profit, not adhering to any social values.

ANALYSIS
After doing a good job with **LifeSkill #1**, Janet understood the various components of the big picture, the overall situation. The "Connections" (**LifeSkill #2: Focus on Connections**) were fairly obvious, but she thought about them anyway. She saw several.

She believed in the Value-Behavior connection (making behavior consistent with values), and, clearly, her values concerning violent toys were being contradicted whenever her job required she promote those toys. She had to decide how important that Value-Behavior connection was to her.

Janet was also aware she was connected to the company as a whole, to her boss, and to the other employees. Except for the manufacture and sale of violent toys, the company did good work in making safe and enjoyable products for children. She wanted the company to be successful with those products. Success would breed a good work atmosphere for all employees, including herself.

Janet spent some time on Friday trying to come up with an action plan. The first idea that popped in her head was to write a memo to Edith Wilson, the president of the company. As President, Edith had the power to initiate major changes at TU. The memo would get the ball rolling on the violent toys issue.

Excited she was taking immediate action, Janet wrote the memo. In it she briefly cited a market research article she had read showing consumers were trending away from violent toys and buying more and more of two other types of toys TU manufactured. The memo also included Janet's statement that she believed the company would improve its credibility and enhance its popularity with parents by redirecting resources from violent toys to the other two types.

Janet took the memo to Edith's secretary at 4:40 p.m., who delivered it to Edith within a few minutes. Edith saw it was from the new CRL in Glen's Client Relations department. Following the company's standard procedure requiring employees to go through department heads, not directly to the president, she did not read the memo. Instead, she called Glen.

Glen immediately went to Janet's office. It was the first time she had seen him angry. He told her to be in his office the first thing Monday morning "to sort out a serious problem you have created." Without further explanation, he stalked out of her office. He had not read the memo, and really didn't care about its contents. His newest employee had gone over his head to the president, a clear violation of established protocol.

ANALYSIS
Janet had been so eager to turn her frustration into decisive

action she did not apply two important LifeSkills.

She did not consider **LifeSkill #3 (Develop Secure I, Secure Other, and Secure We)**. She was so new on the job she had not had enough time to establish a "secure we" relationship with Glen, and certainly not with Edith. Glen appreciated Janet's hard work, the way she dealt with clients, and her admirable team spirit, but that did not mean he had a secure relationship with her. Furthermore, Edith had never even had a conversation with Janet.

Another problem was Janet's lack of attention to **LifeSkill #4: Clarify**. When she was first hired, she went through the one-day orientation required of all new employees. The orientation manual included a sentence that read, "Any concerns an employee has relating to the company are to be expressed in a concise memo to the appropriate department director."

At the time, Janet privately thought the directive was a bit vague. For example, what should an employee do if the "concern" focused on the behavior of a department director? Where should the memo be sent in such a case? Furthermore, Edith had told the new employees she had an "open door" policy, and was available if employees wanted to communicate directly with her. Janet saw some contradiction between the directive and the open door policy. However, she had not asked for clarification during orientation, nor in the month since orientation.

Unaware she had failed to consider the LifeSkills mentioned above, Janet spent a portion of the weekend preparing for her Monday morning meeting with Glen. She wondered if he was angry because he and Edith had read the memo and opposed its suggestions, or if his anger stemmed from the vague directive having being violated and the memo bypassing him and going directly to the president. Either way, Janet worried she might be fired.

Janet's preparation wisely included **LifeSkill #5: What Needs To Be Done, What Can Be Done, and How To Do It**. She considered each of the three parts of the LifeSkill, and here's what emerged.

What Needs To Be Done

(1) She needed to keep her job.
(2) She needed to clarify why she was in trouble.
(3) If she was in trouble because she violated the vague directive,

she needed to apologize for going over Glen's head and explain why she did it.

(4) If she was in trouble because of the content of the memo, she would need to make sure her proposal concerning violent toys was clearly expressed, including why implementing the proposal would be good for the company.

(5) She needed to get clarification on the vague directive for the sake of other employees who might be in a similar situation in the future.

What Can Be Done

Janet felt she was capable of doing everything on her "needs to be done" list. How Glen and Edith eventually responded was not within her power to determine. The need to show how her proposal would benefit the company required more research, which she could do. So she spent some of the weekend looking at additional market research data and the company's published sales reports for the past five years.

(The **How To Do It** part of LifeSkill #5 flows seamlessly into **LifeSkill #6, Focus on Process and Develop "Doables"**. We will resume our eavesdropping on the Monday morning meeting to see what happened. The entire meeting shows Janet's use of How To Do It, and Focus on Process and Develop "Doables.)

Glen was waiting for her when Janet entered his office at 8:30 a.m. The expression on his face reminded her of a storm cloud getting ready to let loose thunder and lightning. She felt herself swallow hard. He motioned for her to sit in a chair. He stayed seated behind his big desk. As she looked across at him, the desk seemed to get even bigger and more imposing

"You have greatly disappointed me," Glen told her. "You violated company policy by sending a memo directly to the president. I'm on the verge of firing you."

(The reason Janet was in trouble was clarified by Glen. She didn't have to do it.)

Although nervous, Janet had to trust in herself and her preparation. "I hope we can find other options. I like my job, I think you and I have worked well together, and I believe I'm an asset to the company. I sincerely apologize for how I handled the memo. I now understand I should have sent it to you."

"Yes, you should have."

"Did you or the president have a chance to read it?"

"I have not read it and neither has the president. The point is you violated company policy. An employee does not bypass her boss and send a memo directly to the president. I find it hard to trust employees who don't follow proper channels."

"I understand, and it won't happen again," Janet said sincerely. "I made a rookie mistake. My only purpose was to contribute some ideas and research I believe can help our company."

Being deeply committed to the success of the company, Glen perked up a bit. He had thought the memo might contain some negative comments about him. But he was still upset Janet had gone over his head. "You've been here only a month. How could you know what's good for the company? You can't even follow proper protocol."

"I've been doing some research on my own time," Janet replied, "mostly studying recent market trends and TU's sales. What I've discovered shows which types of toys are selling well and which are not, and how that trend will continue."

ANALYSIS

Glen has been fixated solely on a "Dot", the fact the memo bypassed him and went directly to the president. Janet is Broadening the Context to include the content of the memo. She is also promoting a "we" and "Power-WITH" atmosphere by using the words "we" and "our company." She is also focusing on an important "connector" they both care about: the success of the company. Glen is being invited to see the bigger picture, and since he didn't get to be Client Relations Director by being narrow-minded, he begins to expand his vision. Furthermore, he knows Janet has been a very good worker in all respects.....except the memo mistake.

"I'm still thinking of firing you," Glen said, "but the president and all the department directors need to be aware of the latest market trends."

"Have you had a chance to look at the memo?"

"No. It was improperly sent."

"Would you take a look at it? I have a copy with me."

"Now why does that not surprise me," he said with a slight hint of a grin. "Let me see it."

She handed it to him and he read it for the next three minutes.

"Hmmm. Interesting. That's never been done before....having such a new employee at your level be involved in a major presentation like this. But I want to get up to speed on the research before moving forward. Leave the additional research with me, and I'll study it today. I have a long meeting with the president scheduled for tomorrow, and I'll add this to the agenda. Then I'll get back to you."

"I appreciate that."

"But the other issue hasn't been resolved. I accept your apology for violating protocol, but you need to make sure never to do it again. And you need to apologize in person to the president."

"I agree, and I'll do it today."

Janet leaves Glen's office, fully aware she did not bring up the issue of the vague directive. She chose not to at this time because the proposal on violent toys was more important. Throwing another potentially controversial issue into the mix would not be effective.

ANALYSIS

Janet used all of the LifeSkills as she worked with Glen in developing and implementing an effective Process.

• She helped Glen feel more secure in their interaction by offering to apologize, by inviting a "we" atmosphere, and by emphasizing the "connector" of TU's success, a goal they both shared.

• She kept focusing on the Broader Context by emphasizing the content of the memo, not just the way it was sent, and by making the company's welfare her major concern.

• Janet promoted a lot of effective clarifying as they discussed the information in the memo and her additional research. She also clarified how her personal values "just happened to coincide" with her proposal, but the important thing was her proposal would help the company.

• "Power-WITH" was in full swing as Glen and Janet talked together about what to do next.

• Several "Doables" were developed. The first was Janet apologizing personally to Edith. The second was that Glen would read the summary of Janet's additional research. That was a very feasible first step which led to the next Doable, his adding the topic to the agenda of his long meeting with Edith the next day. The larger step, meeting with the appropriate personnel, flowed naturally from those first two Doables.

The meeting was held the next week, and Edith invited Janet to make a presentation on her research. The Research Department was tasked to verify Janet's findings, and found they were accurate. Edith then set in motion a six month process to shift a percentage of the resources that had been devoted to violent toys to the other two types the research clearly showed were increasing in consumer popularity.

Mutual Benefit Outcomes clearly emerged from the effective Process.

Within a year, the company had increased profits, some going into an improved health care package for the employees. The Research Department was enlarged to keep more current on market trends. Janet brought up the vague directive in a meeting with Glen, and when Edith became involved, the directive was clarified and revised.

As for Janet, the benefits she received were spinoffs from her excellent work. She kept her job, of course, reconnected her values with her behavior....and even got a raise.

Chapter 8:   The Caldwell Family

AUTHOR'S NOTE: This case is taken from an actual situation I experienced a couple of years ago. Only the names have been changed.

We begin with a brief introduction of the Caldwell family. A more thorough description will be provided a little later.

Mother and wife Ann works as a high school science teacher. Father and husband Jeff owns and manages a small, struggling company of twelve employees. Their son Mike, 16, is going through the usual highs and lows teenagers experience. Daughter Tami, 15, has become what Ann calls, "the glue holding the family together."

Tami attended a youth workshop I conducted on December 1. She became very interested in applying the LifeSkills in what she called her "dysfunctional family". The next week, she read the book you are now reading, and called me at my office. She would like to organize a family meeting, something never before experienced by the family as a whole.

I encouraged her to give it a good try, and she mentioned the idea to the family a day later. They thought such a meeting wasn't needed and even seemed a bit strange. Mike also said it was just another of Tami's crazy ideas to keep her busy because she didn't have a current boyfriend.

So by December 6, Tami had not been able to organize a family meeting. Then several events occurred during the next few days that would bring things to a head. The first event took place at dinner on December 8.

Dinners in the Caldwell household were usually rushed affairs without much conversation. If an enterprising nutrition guru were to create a magical pill that could serve as an alternative to sitting at the table and eating dinner as a family, the Caldwells would definitely choose the pill. Not having such a choice, the family must be content to gather at the table and eat dinner the conventional way.

And that's where the Caldwells were on December 8, eating dinner in their usual silence. (Tami described what happened at the dinner when she called me at my office the next day.)

As they ate in silence, Tami suddenly initiated conversation. "Do you think we're a dysfunctional family?" she asked.

Chewing stopped. Jeff and Ann looked at each other, both

hesitating in hopes the other would come up with an appropriate response. Mike's attention was focused on devouring his food as quickly as possible, except for the broccoli. He wanted to go to his room and play video games.

Tami tried again. "I read an article in the school library today on dysfunctional families. I think it described us....individually and together. I think if we had that family meeting I've been suggesting, it would help."

"Mike, stop eating like a pig," Jeff said, not wanting to deal Tami's question. "And you haven't touched your broccoli."

"You know I hate broccoli."

"Let's just have a nice dinner," Ann smiled at Tami. "We can talk about your question later if you still want to."

Silence filled the rest of dinner time. And that gives us an opening to learn about the family in greater detail before getting to the next event of that important week.

Jeff. Jeff's favorite lament to anyone who will listen goes something like this. "Living these days is like trying to fly in the middle of a tornado. Nothing seems to be effective, not at home, not at work, not anywhere."

Jeff blames it all on various culprits. The government.... dirty tricks done by his business competitors.....global terrorism....illegal immigration.....his own employees....the terrible teens Mike and Tami are going through....Jeff's list of who and what's to blame goes on and on. He does not want to consider the possibility that some of his ineffectiveness might be attributed to his own lack of dependable skills for making decisions, dealing with problems and conflicts, and interacting well at home and at work.

Ann. Ann pictures her current life as a puzzle containing a zillion pieces, and the task of living requires putting the pieces together in the proper arrangement. But there are no instructions and no picture of what the whole puzzle is supposed to look like when assembled correctly. She blames a lot of it on the educational system that fails to teach youth any principles and skills for making good decisions, but she's not sure what those principles and skills should be, or if any dependable ones actually exist. She feels powerless to change the educational system because, as she puts it, "I am just a lowly science teacher." She also feels ineffective when she tries to protect her teenagers from succumbing to some of the most alluring temptations of the contemporary youth culture. As for her relationship with husband Jeff, well, she just feels "it is what it is" and doesn't spend a lot of time figuring out what that means.

Mike. Mike, 16, is perceived by Jeff as being like a confused dog on a leash, led around by teenage misfits who only want to cause trouble, thumb their noses at authority, and experiment with anything adults deem as "inappropriate". Mike resents being perceived that way, and sees himself as a kid who is just trying to enjoy his teenage years before the heavy responsibilities of adulthood descend upon him. He feels a kind of simmering anger at adults because they have made a mess of the world he is being forced to inherit. He doesn't have a clue there might be effective LifeSkills he can learn and apply.

Tami. Tami, 15, is very popular, makes excellent grades in school, is involved in many extra-curricular activities, and never causes much trouble at home. Ann wonders if one of the reasons Tami causes so little trouble at home is because she's hardly ever there. Ann and Jeff have convinced themselves their daughter isn't home very much because she's extremely busy with school activities. She is, but there is another reason. Tami feels the family is seriously "dysfunctional" (one of her most profound new words), and she finds herself getting frustrated when she's at home in that kind of environment...especially since the other members of the family don't seem to realize the family is indeed dysfunctional.

By Friday, December 11, neither Tami nor her parents had initiated further conversation on the "dysfunctional family" topic, which Tami felt was one more sign of how dysfunctional they all were. Ann and Jeff organized a birthday party at their house for one of their friends, and, under strong begging from Mike and Tami, agreed to allow them to go to their own separate parties the same night. Both of the parties were chaperoned by adults Ann and Jeff knew fairly well.

The family had only one car, so Jeff dropped off Tami and Mike at their respective parties then returned home for the birthday celebration. The agreement was that Mike and Tami would call home no later than 11:30, and either Jeff or Ann would go pick them up.

The birthday party at the Caldwell house ended at 11:00, and all the guests left. At 11:15, the telephone rang. Ann answered and was greatly surprised the caller was the school district's lawyer. He told her an organization calling itself PATE (Parents for Truth in Education) had just made charges against Ann for "teaching un-Christian beliefs" during a lesson she had given the past week. The topic of the lesson was the formation of the Earth and the evolution of Homo sapiens.

Ann had introduced the lesson by saying all people had a right to their religious beliefs, that religion was important but different than science, and that all she was doing was teaching what science had thus far proven to be factual. Still, the PATE group was demanding the school board revoke Ann's teaching credentials and also ban such lessons throughout the school district. The group was even threatening to hold demonstrations in front of the school and Ann's home.

Ann was shocked and knew the situation was serious or else the lawyer would not have called so late on a Friday night. She looked for Jeff and found him out on the front porch alone, obviously worrying about something. When she told him what the lawyer had said, he did not respond with the deep level of concern Ann was hoping for and needing. Instead, he said, "Let the lawyer handle it. I've got my own problems to worry about."

Jeff was mostly fixating on the fact his business was in deep trouble. Sales had fallen a whopping 40% from the previous year. Depressing visions swirled in his head as he imagined bankruptcy, having to sell the house and cars, and the shame of being seen as an impotent provider for his family. To make matters worse, one of his most annoying business competitors who came to the birthday party had gloated loudly, "Jeff's business will go belly up this year." At least a dozen of Jeff's friends heard the comment.

Cleaning up after the birthday party was the last thing on their minds. Jeff headed to his study to sulk about his business woes, and Ann headed to the den to work herself into a frenzy about PATE's threats and her future as a teacher. They were so preoccupied with their own troubles, neither realized 11:30 had passed, then 11:45, and Mike and Tami had not called.

A knock was heard on the front door. When Jeff opened it, there was Mike flanked by two detectives. They said a violent incident had occurred outside the house where Mike's party was held and he was under suspicion for having taken part. He would have to appear before a juvenile court judge in two days to determine if charges would be brought. Before leaving, the detectives said Mike was under orders not to leave the house until the court appearance.

Seeing their son reminded them they also had a daughter, and she had not called. Ann called Tami's cell phone, nobody answered, and Ann left a voice message. Then she found the phone number of the place Tami's party was supposed to be held, called, and was told Tami had left at a little before 10:00.

When Ann told Jeff, he seemed not to hear her. How could he?

He was busy yelling at Mike for causing problems "at a time my company is in ruins!" Mike was off in his own world wondering how his young life had become so complicated and how he would get out of the latest mess he was in.

Ann slumped in a chair feeling the weight of the world on her shoulders. Her son might be arrested, her daughter's whereabouts were still unknown, and Jeff had made a mess of his business and seemed to think that was the only problem facing the family.

Then, as mothers are prone to do even in somewhat dysfunctional families, Ann pulled herself together and focused on the most needed and immediate task. Find Tami.

A bright idea came to her. Call Debra, Tami's best friend, who was probably at the same party Tami had attended. Debra answered her cell phone after numerous rings. In a sleepy voice she said Tami was with her, and handed her the phone.

"We didn't like the party and came here a little after ten," Tami explained. "I know I should have called, but we fell asleep watching a movie on TV. Sorry, Mom. Can I stay the rest of the night here? I'm really tired. Debra's mother said she'll take me home at eight in the morning after I have breakfast here."

Ann was angry, but Tami was safe and that was most important. "I called you on your cell. Why didn't you answer?"

"I fell asleep. That vibrator humming thing isn't much use unless I'm sleeping on top of the phone, which I wasn't. I need to get one with a ring or music."

"Well, I'll let you stay the night, but you should have called."

"How's everybody else doing?" Tami asked.

"If I told you, you'd just say we're a dysfunctional family and I don't want to hear that because you're right. Things are in a horrible mess but I'm too stressed to talk about it now."

"We'll all be at home tomorrow so let's get together and sort things out. I know each of us has our own problems, but we need to start working together, Mom. We're going to fall apart if we don't. We need to have that family meeting....like tomorrow."

"I feel the same way. But let's have the meeting after lunch so we can all sleep late. We need to be rested. See you tomorrow."

Ann hung up, wondering how Tami could have turned out so wise, given the household she grew up in.

When Ann reported what Tami had said, Mike saw an opportunity to shift attention off his questionable behavior of the evening while at the same time making Tami look bad. He liked to get his "perfect" sister in trouble, and jumped at the latest chance. "You always believe her and never believe me," he grumped. "Maybe she's lying. Maybe she got drunk at the party and was wandering around on some street corner and Debra's mom had to sober her up."

Ann glared at him, and before she could say anything, Mike headed for his room. "I'm tired and I'm going to bed."

Jeff pounced, verbally at least. "You show up with detectives and think you can just slink off to bed?"

"Let's talk about everything tomorrow when we're thinking more clearly," Ann wisely suggested. "We can all sleep late then we'll meet in the den after lunch. It's long overdue."

The morning arrived, and when Tami came home at eight she found the rest of the family sleeping. She was thankful she had the entire morning to prepare for the meeting. She knew she would have to take the lead if anything constructive would result. The fact she was only fifteen didn't matter. She reminded herself that age is just a number.

Applying the LifeSkills at the Caldwell Family Meeting

Tami spent the morning in her room reviewing the LifeSkills and planning what she would do at the meeting. When Ann awoke, Tami convinced her it would be a good idea to tape the meeting. Tami felt it would help them remember "who does what by when" if they were able to develop a process for improving the family situation.

(NOTE: A week after the meeting, Tami and the family allowed me to hear the tape and use the contents as a case study for this book..... provided their names be changed.)

Here are excerpts from the meeting, taken verbatim from the tape. We will use a dialogue format with T=Tami, A=Ann, J=Jeff, and M=Mike. As we go through the meeting, you and I will take "pauses" to analyze how the LifeSkills are being applied.

(The family gathers in the den after lunch. Jeff really doesn't want to be there, but comes so he can impress upon the family the seriousness of his company's problems. Ann is there because she wants to support Tami's brave initiative, and because the family is in a mess. And Mike? He's there because Ann said he had to be, plus, he's curious to see what his weird sister has planned and if she can pull it off.)

T: Is it okay if I----

J: (wanting to assert his authority as the so-called head of the household before his teenage daughter takes charge) Tami, that stunt you pulled last night, not calling us.... don't ever do that again!
T: I won't, Dad, and I apologize for worrying you and Mom. Is it okay if I start things off in our meeting?"
A: Nobody else seems to want to, and, anyway I think you're the one to do it.
T: Dad? Okay with you?
J: Sure, why not.
T: Mike?
M: How long is this going to take?
T: I'm sure you have some good contributions to make. We all do. So let's just spend whatever time we need to. And we can take breaks. (Tami has prepared four pieces of paper, each one with the Circle & Dot drawing. She hands them out.)
T: The Circle represents the bigger picture of what we're dealing with as a family. There are a lot of things in the Circle. Let's each of us say what we think some of those things are. (Tami thinks Ann is the most willing to try, so turns to her) Mom? Why don't you go first and mention a couple of the things you see as important.
A: Okay. I think the most important part of the bigger picture is finding a way we can all work together better as a family. A second thing is the trouble I've got at school with this PATE organization. That's the big thing for me. You want me to explain that now?
T: Let's let Dad and Mike mention a couple of things they see in the bigger picture, then we'll clarify any that need clarifying. Dad? A couple of things?
J: Well, all I know is we're in a hell of a mess. My company is hurting, and that's the priority. And my wife is being targeted by a bunch of fanatics......my son is in trouble with the law..... and---
M: Don't blame me for the fix we're in. And I didn't do what the cops think I did at the party. I'm being framed. That's the main thing going on.
T: We'll get to that for sure. Mike, what else do you see we're dealing with as a family?
M: I get confused about what's expected of me. I never know what chores I'm supposed to do around the house, then when I don't

T: do one I never knew I was supposed to do, Dad jumps all over me. (He looks at Tami.) You haven't said what you think are parts of this Circle thing. If I have to go along with this...this game of yours, you should have to, too.

T: It's not a game, but you're right, I need to mention some things I see. The things everybody has mentioned, I see those, too. Plus, I think we need to do more of what we're doing right now.... working through the various things that affect us all. And we need to do it together and regularly.

M: You mean more family meetings? I'm not so sure about that.

T: How do you feel about this one so far?

M: (pause) Well...I guess it's a little more interesting than I thought it would be. I was expecting everybody would jump on me about last night.

T: I think the important thing is that we are all in this together. Everything we have mentioned affects us all, and we can all be ready and willing to help each other deal with those things. Nobody has to do it alone. We need each other, and we have each other.

(Tami refers back to the Circle & Dot handouts.)

T: The Dot in the Circle refers to something a person might be fixating on to the exclusion of everything else in the Circle. The Dots are very important, of course, but they are not the only important thing. What do you see as some Dots?

A: I guess you mean something like my making the PATE issue the only thing.

J: And fixating on my company. But just remember that's a very important issue.

M: Is my being framed for the fight at the party a Dot?

T: It is if you think only about that one thing and ignore the other things that affect all of us.

Pause for Analysis of LifeSkills #1, #2, and #3.
LifeSkill #1: Focus on the Broader Context
(the Circle, not just the Dots)

Identifying the components in the Circle has already helped the entire family see the bigger picture, not only their own particular Dots. Let's summarize the components of the Broader Context the family has

identified.
- The reality the family must pull together to deal with their situation even though they have not been able to work together effectively in the past. At least two specifics have emerged, including (a) confused expectations of each other, and (b) a lack of regular and effective communication.
- The violence at the party and Mike's possible role.
- The PATE group and what it is doing.
- The problems in Jeff's company.

Before "filling in the Circle" at the meeting, Jeff, Mike, and to some degree Ann were mostly fixating on their respective Dots. Jeff on the poor state of his business, Mike on his trouble with the law, and Ann on the PATE crisis. Tami doesn't seem to have a Dot, yet she will need to be careful not to assume her enthusiasm over using the LifeSkills will be shared enthusiastically by the other members of the family. That could lead to (a) unrealistic expectations on her part; and/or (b) becoming lax in emphasizing the LifeSkills because she assumes the other members understand them and are committed to using them; and/or (c) giving up if they aren't using the LifeSkills.

LifeSkill #2: Focus on Connections

Tami has introduced and affirmed "connections" and "connectors" without even using those words. She has done it through comments, such as, "We are all in this together", "Everything we have mentioned affects us all", and "We can all be willing and able to help each other". Continuing to emphasize such concepts is especially important because the family has a pattern of being "disconnected" from each other.

LifeSkill #3: Develop Secure I. Secure Other, Secure We

Many people seem to assume a family, just because they are a family, will have a Secure I, a Secure Other, and a Secure We in their interactions with each other. The Caldwells clearly demonstrate such an assumption can be faulty.

Several things Tami has done thus far have planted the seeds for stronger feelings of being secure without ever using the word "secure". For example: (1) Everybody has participated equally in the discussion. (2) Nobody's comments have been ignored or treated as insignificant. (3) Tami's comment, "We aren't alone in dealing with any of these situations. We need each other and we have each other." All of these contributions help lay a foundation on which Secure I, Secure Other, and Secure We can be developed.

T: Let's return to the meeting. We've helped each other see the bigger picture, and now I think it would be good if we clarified some of the things in that bigger picture. Of the things that need clarifying, which is the most urgent and most feasible?

J: We need to get Mike's side of the story of what happened at the party, then we need to figure out who these fanatics are in that PATE group. My company problems will take longer to sort out. So...what happened at the party, Mike? And don't lie to me, son.

M: Some guys who weren't invited showed up, picked a fight on the lawn outside, and me and Tim tried to break it up. I wasn't fighting, I was trying to stop the fight. A neighbor had called the police even before the fight started, and the cops were so stupid they didn't even try to figure out what was happening. They just jumped to conclusions.

A: Surely there are witnesses who can support your innocence. Should we get a lawyer to represent Mike, go talk to the witnesses, get statements, and present them to the Judge?

M: Good idea, Mom. The cops should have done that on the spot.

T: What's next? The PATE thing? I've never heard of that group. What's their deal, Mom? Why are they after you?
(Ann explained the situation fully, so Tami moved on.)

T: Dad? Do we want to clarify anything about the company?

J: I need to go over the finances again tomorrow. I'll let everybody know if I come up with anything you can do to help.

Pause for Analysis of LifeSkill # 4
LifeSkill #4: Clarify

Tami initiated the timing and use of LifeSkill #4 very well. Although most people know intellectually that clarifying is important, it is often neglected. Tami made sure it was used in a very clear and obvious way.

It's interesting and instructive to observe how Jeff is getting into the process. Rather than hanging on to his company's woes as the only vital issue, he suggested focusing on clarifying Mike's situation first, then Ann's, before discussing the company. Tami helped promote Jeff's doing so by asking, "What is the most <u>urgent</u> and most <u>feasible</u> thing we need to clarify?" Asking questions rather than just making statements always helps the clarification process, as Tami is demonstrating.

    We return to the meeting.
T: We've clarified some things and looked at what needs to be done, so let's see what we <u>can</u> do.....what we are capable of doing ourselves, and what we aren't capable of doing and probably need some help from outside the family.
J: Well, in Mike's case, I can call John Rollins when we take a break. The family can't go around talking to witnesses but his investigators can. He's handled juvenile cases before, and he's a good friend. He'll represent Mike and won't charge much.
T: Is there anything I can do to help with Mike's situation? I mean, I can stand by you, Mike, and I will 100%, and not just because you're my brother. You're not a person who gets into fights. But is there anything else I can do?
M: I'm not even sure what I can do about my mess. I guess that sounds lame, but....
J: You can think about your presentation to the judge. Your Mom and Tami can help. They're better at that sort of thing than I am.
T: Mike? How does all this sound?
M: Good. Thanks everybody.
T: Now, what about Mom's case? What can we for sure do?
A: During our break I can call the school district lawyer to find out if the district is supporting me, and if he thinks PATE really has enough power to get me fired.
T: And I can look on the Internet to see if PATE has a web page. It will probably list their leaders and tell something about their overall goals.
J: Can we get the police or the school board to do something if this bunch of fanatics really do demonstrate in front of our house?
A: I can ask the lawyer about that.
T: Dad, about the company... I think we all want to help, but just speaking for myself, I'm not sure I know enough. One small thing is maybe Mike and I can cut back on buying things we don't really need. Right, Mike?
M: (with a little grin) If you say so, Miss Chairperson. Hey, I know how I can help with the company. I can help Dad go over the finances.
    (Everybody laughs, well aware of Mike's low grades in math.)

T: Is this a good time to take a break so we can do the things we said we need to do? How about taking an hour? Do we need to remind ourselves who will do what?

J: Good idea. Let's take turns. I'm calling John Rollins to get help with Mike's case.

A: I'm calling the school's lawyer.

T: And I'm researching PATE on the Internet.

M: And I'm playing video games. Only kidding. I'm going to work on how I'm going to tell what happened to the judge. And I think I should call Tim and find out what his parents are doing. He's sort of in the same fix I'm in. Like I said, he helped me stop the fight. Or we tried to, at least.

J: After you call him, it might be good if I talked with his father. Maybe we can coordinate our efforts.

T: Can we do all this in an hour, then come back and discuss what's next?

A: Absolutely. (Jeff and Mike agree)

Pause for Analysis of LifeSkill #5 and #6

LifeSkill #5: Focus on What Needs To Be Done, Can Be Done, and How To Do It

What Needs To Be Done

In any situation, some important needs will always be revealed through the use of the first four LifeSkills. This has certainly happened at the Caldwell family meeting. Let's review the needs they have already identified.

In Mike's situation, his explanation of what happened at the party was a definite need. Another was finding witnesses to support his innocence. Yet another was obtaining a lawyer to help make Mike's case in court if needed.

Getting more information on PATE and talking with the school lawyer were two important needs relating to Ann's situation.

Within the context of a family, each of those needs clearly affects every member. What Tami has done thus far has helped establish that very important fact.

It is important to emphasize another point. To Tami, simply having the meeting was a need, not just a nice exercise with uncertain possibilities. As the LifeSkills were used, Jeff, Ann and Mike began to come to the same conclusion. Furthermore, recognition of the need to improve the family's overall situation led to the important realization of another need: working <u>together</u>. Without it, the family's situation will not be improved.

What **C**an Be Done

With practical, effective skills in their hands, the family discussed what they themselves are capable of doing and not doing. Each family member found something he or she could realistically contribute. Furthermore, they wisely avoided taking on any tasks they were not equipped to handle, and they realized which tasks needed help from outside sources (such as witnesses at Mike's party, John Rollins, and the school district's lawyer).

<u>H</u>ow To Do It

In one sense, the entire meeting has been an example of "How To Do It". Why? Because Tami, from the very beginning, promoted a process that was based on the LifeSkills.

More specific aspects of "how-to" emerged, especially the development and use of "Power-WITH". As the meeting progressed, the concept of "we" and "our working together" gained strength. Any attempts to engage in battles for "power-over" each other, or even thoughts of "my power alone", were seen correctly as counter-productive.

In any situation where the LifeSkills are being used effectively, the <u>H</u>ow To Do It part of LifeSkill #5 always blends with all the others in a seamless process. The blending together of "how to do it" with LifeSkill #6 is the most obvious. So let's move to that LifeSkill in our analysis as the family takes its important, busy, one-hour break.

LifeSkill #6: Focus on Process and Develop "Doables"

The key ingredients of this LifeSkill are (1) effective process; (2) Doables; (3) The Three W's (Who Does What by When); (4) mutual benefit outcomes; (5) sustainability; and (6) structural and systemic considerations.

1. Effective Process. As mentioned earlier, the Focus on Process was established by Tami at the very beginning of the meeting. In a relaxed, "we're in this together" tone, she invited and energized <u>a process based on the LifeSkills</u>. As almost always happens when the LifeSkills are used, the people involved in an interaction realize the practical and effective power of the Process being created. They become willing and active participants in implementing the Process, as we saw in the Caldwell family meeting.

2. Doables. Developing feasible, practical steps ("Doables") is always a major element in any effective Process, and Tami helped the family find and act on several Doables.

One of the valuable functions of a Doable is that it helps build momentum and confidence. That means a few Doables need to be implemented early, rather than waiting to take action until a long list of Doables has been compiled. Another function of a Doable, a "steppingstone", is that it can lead to and help determine additional steps in the building of an effective pathway toward effective outcomes. The family did an excellent job of fulfilling those two functions by taking a break to implement a few of the most feasible Doables before further complicating their situation.

3. Who Does What by When. Tami made sure the Three W's were not overlooked. Actually using the words "Who Does What by When" is always helpful. Tami used those words and even had each member of the family summarize the tasks each would do during the break.

We will wait to examine the other ingredients of LifeSkill #6 (Mutual Benefit Outcomes, Sustainability, and Structural Considerations) until the family meeting concludes.

(The family comes back together after the break and reports on the tasks they completed and the information they gathered.)

T: Let's report on what we found out during the break. Dad?
J: I talked with John Rollins and he gladly agreed to help with Mike's case. He'll come over early tomorrow and we'll all develop a strategy. I also talked with Tim's father, and we asked John to take on Tim's case as well, and he agreed.
M: I worked on my statement to the judge, Tami helped some, and I talked to Tim. He'll need to make a statement, too, and he's working on it.
T: Mom?
A: After Tami got some information from the Internet about PATE, I called the school district's lawyer. He said the school board was determined not to be pushed around by PATE, and that I'm not in danger of being fired. But he felt there was nothing the school district could do if PATE made good on the threat

to demonstrate outside our house. He said if any trouble occurred, the police would have to deal with it.

T: Is there anything else we need to do right now, and can do? Dad, I don't want us to forget about the company. You said you need to go over the finances. Can we get together after you do and see if the rest of us can do anything to help?

J: Definitely. I'll work some tomorrow on it, then after Mike goes to court I'll let you know. We can all meet again. And, speaking of this family meeting idea, I was skeptical about it, as you know, Tami. But I have to admit it makes a lot of sense. It has been very helpful. I'd even be willing to do it regularly, not just wait until we have a crisis.

A: I agree wholeheartedly. Oh, before I forget. I have one other thing to mention. My type of situation might happen to some other teacher unless the district establishes a clear policy about certain topics we cover in science courses. I should have mentioned that to the lawyer. I'll do it later today.

T: Before we end our meeting there's something Mike said a week or so ago I think we need to deal with. It's about his feeling unsure what's expected of him in chores around the house. I feel the same way. What do we need to do about that?

A: I say we come up with a kind of schedule. Most families probably have one of those.

T: I suggest we do it together....like we're doing on all these other things.

J: Okay. I'll get us together in...let's say three days. After these other things are done.

T: How does that sound, Mike?

M: Sounds good.

A: (taking a deep breath and letting it out) Tami? You did a great job with this meeting.

T: Thanks, but we all did it together.

M: I must admit it wasn't too bad. Actually, it was kind of interesting. We did great, huh?
So I guess we're finished. Good. I'm starving. What's for dinner?

A: A big bowl of broccoli.

M: Uh.....maybe I'm not so hungry after all.

Finishing our analysis of the ingredients of LifeSkill #6 requires we skip ahead to a week after the family meeting.

Mike and Tim were cleared of any wrongdoing.

The PATE group, realizing they could not get Ann fired, settled for a small demonstration outside the school. The school board issued a clear policy supporting the teaching of scientific facts as Ann had done in her lesson.

Jeff examined the company's finances and reported back at the second family meeting. Ann said the wife of one of her teaching colleagues was a highly respected financial consultant, and Jeff made an appointment.

The family decided to have a family meeting every two weeks. Tami would serve as the "chairperson" for the next two meetings to serve as an example, then after that each member would take a turn as chairperson.

Continuing our analysis of LifeSkill #6.........

4. Mutual Benefit Outcomes.
Effective outcomes emerge from effective process. So it is no wonder effective and mutually beneficial outcomes resulted. The family used all of the LifeSkills and worked together. The outcomes benefitted, and will continue to benefit, each member and the family as a whole. The outcomes will need to be sustained, the next ingredient of LifeSkill #6.

5. Sustainability. Outcomes are most sustainable when several important criteria are met.
- The process used to reach the outcomes is based on the LifeSkills.
- Follow-up steps to the outcomes are developed and implemented.
- All the parties directly involved have a role in designing and implementing the outcomes.
- If the parties directly involved in a situation cannot do certain tasks by themselves, outside resources are brought in and utilized. Ego, pride, and a stubborn "I can do that" lack of realism cannot be allowed to take hold.

The Caldwell family met all of these criteria. The outcomes they reached stand an excellent chance of being sustainable.

There is a final criteria of sustainability: structural and systemic considerations must be taken into account. It becomes the sixth ingredient of LifeSkill #6.

6. Structural and Systemic considerations. Every action, every outcome exists within certain structures and systems. Ignoring that fact leads to ineffectiveness. Many structures and systems are in need of significant change. I believe we should do all we can to accomplish those changes.

However, if the success of an action or outcome depends on those changes being made, we might be in trouble. It is never wise to put ourselves in such a tenuous position. If we do, we need to make sure and apply the **"What If Step"** in Chapter 1 (planning for various outcomes) and have alternatives in place if the structures and systems cannot be changed.

Three examples from the Caldwell case show how the family realized and acted upon the importance of structural and systemic factors.

One, the family members committed themselves to regular family meetings in the future. That is a "structure/system" that will serve them well.

Two, Ann recognized the need for the school system to formulate a clear policy on the content of science courses, a kind of content structure in which teachers could operate with more clarity and security.

Three, they all worked together to draw up a more organized schedule (a structure) for household chores.

Brief Epilogue

The Caldwell family case happened two years prior to the completion of this book. I have kept up with the family, and it would be unkind of me to leave you wondering about their current state. So here is what has happened in the intervening two years.

The regular family meetings continued, and, miracles of miracles, Mike was often the one who reminded everybody else not to skip any meetings. He gained a new appreciation of his sister because of the original family meeting, and their relationship improved greatly.

Jeff's meeting with the financial advisor Ann recommended proved quite successful. She made several critical suggestions that helped Jeff gain a new way of determining which of his products to drop and which to enhance with shifted resources. He also began using the LifeSkills in improving his role as Boss and his relations with his employees.

Ann continued to teach, and was elected by her peers to be the faculty representative in dealings with the administration and the school board.

The schedule of household chores worked well, with a few hiccups, of course.

And Tami? She had become so interested in the LifeSkills, she wanted to go through one of my training-of-trainers workshops. Needless to say, I was pleased. By the time this book went to print, she had conducted three youth workshops.

Chapter 9: A Neighborhood in Trouble

(NOTE: A slightly different format will be used in this chapter. As we go through what happened in the case, we will pause periodically to give you an opportunity to suggest how the LifeSkills are being used or should be used. I will ask you questions, and after you do some thinking on your own, I will offer my comments.)

The neighborhood known as Riverville is "devouring itself". At least that's the way Nora Eads frequently expresses it. Nora is the organizer and President of a ten-member group self-named, "The Neighborhood Protectors" (NPs). Some of Riverville's more outspoken citizens say "NP" should stand for "Nora's Puppies". Nora handpicked all the members, mostly because they agreed to let her be firmly in charge.

As the President of the NPs, Nora is definitely in her element. All her life she has craved to be in charge of things. Anything. But it's rarely happened. And the few things she has been in charge of have ended up as disasters. Unhappy, unfulfilled, and sincerely worried about her neighborhood, fifty year-old Nora created the unofficial NPs as her chance to be in charge of something worthwhile. She dubbed the members of the NPs "my foot soldiers".

Nora's frequent comments about the neighborhood "devouring itself" are intended as a wake-up call to the citizens. Given the fact that Riverville has, until recently, always been a rather sleepy and tranquil neighborhood, the wake-up call has had no more impact than an alarm clock without sound. The lack of response has frustrated Nora for weeks, agitated her as well, so she often sits in her modest home worrying about the changes in the neighborhood that are causing the "devouring" phenomenon. Daily, she contemplates the list of neighborhood problems.

One, numerous young families, some racially mixed, have moved into Riverville during the past year, living side by side with fourth-generation older families who believe people develop best by "staying with their own kind", especially in terms of race.

Two, two youth gangs have recently formed. Incidents of violence are beginning to make everybody nervous and frightened.

Three, some teenage drug dealers, interpreting in their own way the American dream of "being successful by getting rich", have taken

Life in the Quality Lane

over street corners, dark alleys, and school yards as their territory. The dealers are pulling in as much as $4,000 per week in sales.

And then there's Clete Timms, the Riverville Sheriff. Clete is a rather grumpy grandfather type, near retirement, and good at giving parking tickets but not much else. The last thing he wants is to spend his two remaining years in office dealing with the new, complicated problems in a neighborhood he feels he no longer understands. During the past month, he has been seen fishing in the river more often than at work in his office at the small, three-cell police station.

Everything came to a head two nights ago A major fight between the two youth gangs resulted in severe injury to a dozen youth and widespread destruction of property. By mid-morning the next day, many citizens were finally beginning to realize the gravity of Riverville's situation. Nora pounced on the opportunity, gathered her Foot Soldiers for a crisis meeting, and insisted Sheriff Timms attend.

Enter Sonja, 26, a young nurse who had attended a community workshop I conducted the previous week on the LifeSkills. Although she was not a member of the Neighborhood Protectors organization, Sonja wanted to attend the meeting and made her wishes known to Nora. Nora was reluctant, but finally agreed, primarily because Sonja had been Riverville High School's Homecoming Queen, a star softball pitcher, and had compiled an outstanding academic record in high school, university, and nursing school. Those things greatly impressed Nora.

Based on the tape recording Nora made, and Sonja's conversations with me afterward, here's an accounting of what happened at the meeting.

"We need to set some objectives and go after them with all our energy," Nora started the meeting. "To have a record, I'm taping what we do here today. Here are the objectives we're going after. One, we will break up the gangs. Two, we will get rid of those awful drug dealers. Three, we will make the races get along with each other. Four, we will recruit twenty people to serve as a volunteer security team of peacekeepers. And five, we will contact the National Guard and have them ready to move in when we call them." She paused, then said passionately, "This is our neighborhood and we can't let it be destroyed!"

With those objectives clear in her own mind, Nora felt she was off to a good start. She was oblivious to the confused expressions on the faces of her Foot Soldiers. Sheriff Clete was in obvious discomfort, too, but Nora didn't notice.

Sonja was sitting off to one side. With the LifeSkills fresh in her mind from the recent workshop, Sonja had decided her contribution would involve interjecting the LifeSkills if they were not being applied. In the privacy of her own thoughts, she quickly assessed things thus far.

(Pause for Analysis)
As Sonja does her assessment, I invite you to do the same.
Question: What is your assessment of Nora's use of the LifeSkills this far?
For example, has she Focused on the Broader Context, and is she fixating on any "Dots"? Has she helped build a Secure We among the people at the meeting? (If "yes", how? If "no", how could she do it better?) In terms of the NCH LifeSkill, what is she already failing to consider?

Author's Comments:
1. Nora seems to have used LifeSkill #1 somewhat by considering the numerous components of the Broader Context, the "Circle", the overall situation in Riverville. She does seem to have a "DOT", however. She seems fixated on her being in charge, which has already led to her choosing as NP's only those citizens who will do her bidding.

2. Nora's comment, "This is our neighborhood" at least hints at LifeSkill #2, Focus on Connections. However, she is not paying much attention to LifeSkill #3, developing a Secure I, Secure Other, and Secure We. The other people at the meeting seem to be feeling overwhelmed by Nora's authoritative style and her listing of grandiose objectives. Furthermore, it is obvious Nora has thus far shown little interest in getting input from the others.

3. Nora does not seem to be focusing on the What CAN Be Done portion of the NCH LifeSkill,, choosing instead to assume the group can do everything that needs to be done. We'll see if that changes.

(Back to the meeting.)
Sonja remained patient, waiting until she felt her contributions could be helpful.
Nora plowed ahead. "Riverville is devouring itself!" Even her favorite line didn't seem to arouse the group, but Nora didn't notice. "I'm assigning two people each to handle each of the objectives. You'll report directly to me. Here are the assignments."
Nora rattled them off. The two people assigned to the youth

gang objective said, in unison, "We don't know anything about youth gangs." One of them added, "Gangs are dangerous. How would we go about breaking up a gang?"

Nora didn't have a clue either, but felt the objective was solid. "Figure out how to do it," she told the two worried assignees. "It's a noble cause, so we can accomplish it."

"We don't have the resources to do some of these objectives," Clete pointed out.

"Then get the resources," Nora told him.

"How? Where? We need a plan, Nora."

Based on the LifeSkills, Sonja assessed what was happening. (I hope you will do the same as we pause again.)

(Pause for analysis)
 Question: Which LifeSkills is Nora ignoring in her latest comments?

(Author's Comments)
1. Questions and comments from the participants are showing the need for LifeSkill #4, Clarify. Nora does not seem aware of the importance of clarification. For example, which of her objectives are most feasible? Which are priorities? Which NP's are best suited for specific objectives and tasks? Where will needed resources come from?

2. As we have seen, Nora has focused on the What Needs To Be Done portion of the LifeSkill #5, but the What Can Be Done portion is in serious need of attention. The comments from the group are questioning whether or not some of the objectives can actually be done by the NP's given current and potential resources. Nora seems to think that isn't important enough to discuss.

3. The comments from the group are focusing first on limitations, not on possibilities. That is probably the result, at least partially, of being loaded down with huge objectives without any thought to developing a wise, effective, practical process.

(Back to the meeting)
Sonja came to the rescue. She looked around at the frustrated group, then at Nora. "Nora? May I make a comment?"

"I'd rather you volunteer for one of the objectives, but....what's your comment?"

"I agree that we have serious problems in the neighborhood.

I'm just concerned that we make sure and use our energy and abilities wisely. I think we need to focus on what we as a small group can actually do well, and, most importantly, how to do it. I think we need to choose an objective we can realistically accomplish, primarily one that expands our resources, then design a process of steps to move us toward that objective."

"All of the objectives need to be accomplished," Nora said impatiently.

"Can this group do them all by ourselves?" Sonja asked.

"No way," Clete interjected. "We would fail and the entire community would get even more discouraged."

"Nora?" Sonja asked. "What about having our first objective be mobilizing the citizens of the neighborhood. It's their community, too. And we need a lot more ideas, skills, and person power than the ten people at this meeting can be expected to provide."

Nora was extremely reluctant to let go of any of her pet objectives, but realized Sonja was making sense. Plus, the other NPs are clearly attracted to Sonja's suggestions. Wanting to remain in charge, Nora realizes she needs to shift gears.

"I guess mobilizing the citizens could be an objective ," Nora said to Sonja. "What do you have in mind?"

"We need a first step to get the process going," Sonja answered, suggesting the need for a good Doable. "I think everybody here probably has some good ideas about what a good first step might be."

"We can get the mayor to hold a neighborhood planning meeting in the high school gym next week," one of the NPs suggested.

The group liked the idea and voiced their support.

"And we need to do some research to prepare," another member added. "Things like....finding out who has influence with the youth gangs....and what the schools, churches and businesses could do to help deal with some of our racial problems."

"And we could recruit the volunteer security peacekeepers at the meeting," Nora chimed in. "That's one of my objectives, remember? So we can have sign-up lists----"

"The last thing we need," Clete interrupted, "is a bunch of untrained vigilantes running around causing even more trouble."

"But---" Nora started to defend her precious objective.

"Maybe," Sonja came to the rescue again, "we need to focus on making the first step--the neighborhood meeting--as effective as possible. I suggest the mayor and Nora co-chair the meeting. If everybody agrees, then we should probably call the mayor and have him join us this morning."

"He'll just want to take charge," Nora said quickly, trying to protect her territory.

Clete rolled his eyes, all too familiar with Nora's "I'm in charge" obsession. Sonja saw him and realized the last thing that was needed was another Clete versus Nora battle. "We're all in this together," Sonja said. "The mayor, Nora, Clete, each of us, our fellow citizens....we all need to be powerful together."

(Pause for analysis)

<u>Task</u>: **Please go through the latest portion of the meeting and identify what you think are the most important LifeSkills Sonja's interventions are energizing.**

(Author's Comments)

1. Sonja has energized the development of an effective <u>process</u>.

2. Nora's "power-over" tendencies have gradually eroded, replaced by "<u>Power-WITH</u>" involving the NP's and the neighborhood as a whole.

3. Sonja asked for the group to come up with a <u>Doable</u>, a good first step. Rather than trying to tackle the vague and numerous objectives all at once (as Nora was more or less suggesting), a feasible beginning to the process emerged. Organizing the Neighborhood Planning Meeting was an ideal Doable. It was feasible, would bring in more people and ideas, and would build momentum.

4. Sonja's comment, "We are all in this together" reinforced the main "connector" among a group that had felt disconnected.

5. A feeling of Secure Self, Secure Other, and Secure We began to replace the insecurity and lack of confidence evident in the group.

6. It is also important to point out how Sonja asked questions to help the members of the group get more involved.

7. And, finally, notice how the NP's began using the LifeSkills themselves. This usually happens in interactions because the LifeSkills make sense, are practical, are effective, and help tasks be done with quality.

(Back to the meeting)

Nora had a dilemma. On one hand, she realized her total domination of the group had disappeared. On the other hand, she realized the group was accomplishing far more by doing things a different way. She saw that her love of the neighborhood and the progress the group was making had greater value than her desire to dominate.

After resisting at first, Nora said, "Okay, I'll call the mayor right now and invite him to join us."

The meeting lasted all day, and at 6 p.m., the specifics of the Neighborhood Planning Meeting, the first step in the process, had been determined. People with critical resources, knowledge, contacts, and skills were called that evening and invited to attend. A Task Force emerged from the Meeting, and the next steps in the process were determined.

Author's Ending Comments

As we have seen throughout the chapters of this book, there are practical LifeSkills we can apply to most any situation and be confident they will add to the quality of our lives. The LifeSkills are down inside us, we are all capable of understanding them and applying them.

They also form the foundation of a process for conflict resolution intervention I call *The Conflict Partnership Catalyst Process*. Professionals such as mediators, and Volunteer conflict resolution interveners as well, can use the CPC Process. Readers interested in the topic can be on the lookout for the forthcoming book on the subject.

I wish each of you well in your many varied experiences and challenges. Your journey can indeed take place in the Quality Lane, and I hope this book can contribute to that end.

Life in the Quality Lane

Made in the USA
Charleston, SC
31 March 2012